Ian Fleming

Twayne's English Authors Series

Kinley E. Roby, Editor

Northeastern University

TEAS 466

IAN FLEMING
(1908–1964)
Photograph courtesy of Times Newspapers Ltd.

Ian Fleming

By Bruce A. Rosenberg

Brown University

Ann Harleman Stewart

Brown University

Twayne Publishers
A Division of G. K. Hall & Co. • *Boston*

Ian Fleming
Bruce A. Rosenberg and Ann Harleman Stewart

Copyright 1989 by G. K. Hall & Co.
All rights reserved.
Published by Twayne Publishers
A Division of G. K. Hall & Co.
70 Lincoln Street
Boston, Massachusetts 02111

Copyediting supervised by Barbara Sutton
Book production by Gabrielle B. McDonald
Book design by Barbara Anderson

Typeset in 11 pt. Garamond
by Compset, Inc., of Beverly, Massachusetts

Printed on permanent/durable acid-free paper
and bound in the United States of America

Library of Congress Cataloging-in-Publication Data

Rosenberg, Bruce A.
    Ian Fleming / by Bruce A. Rosenberg, Ann Harleman Stewart.
        p.   cm.—(Twayne's English authors series ; TEAS 466)
    Bibliography: p.
    Includes index.
    ISBN 0-8057-6977-3 (alk. paper)
    1. Fleming, Ian, 1908–1964—Criticism and interpretation.   2. Spy
stories, English—History and criticism.   3. Bond, James (Fictitious
character) I. Stewart, Ann Harleman.   II. Title.   III. Series.
PR6056.L4Z84   1989
823′.914—dc19   88-37583
                                                                                    CIP

To our parents and our children

Contents

About the Authors
Preface
Chronology

    Chapter One
    The Making of James Bond's Reputation   1

    Chapter Two
    Ian Fleming: A Personality Profile   11

    Chapter Three
    Fleming's Life as a Spy   24

    Chapter Four
    Ian Fleming, Writer   38

    Chapter Five
    Live Sources, Paper Imitations   54

    Chapter Six
    James Bond and the Modern Spy Novel   71

    Chapter Seven
    Bond, Women, and Wogs   87

    Chapter Eight
    Fleming's Villains   106

    Chapter Nine
    Ian Fleming: The Final Report   119

Works Cited   137
Index   141

About the Authors

Bruce A. Rosenberg is professor of American Civilization and English literature at Brown University. He has written books on folklore topics, notably *The Art of the American Folk Preacher* (1970), which won the James Russell Lowell Prize for that year and was reissued in revised form in 1988 as *Can These Bones Live*. His interest in the lore of the American West is reflected in *Custer and the Epic of Defeat* (1975) and *The Code of the West* (1981). *The Spy Story* (1987), co-written with John Cawelti, established his interest in espionage fiction and paved the way for this study of Fleming. He is also the author of more than sixty articles on *Beowulf*, Chaucer, folklore and literature, and the American West. At various times since 1969 he has been a Fellow of the American Council of Learned Societies, the National Endowment for the Humanities, the Newberry Library, the Henry E. Huntington Library, and the John Simon Guggenheim Foundation.

Ann Harleman Stewart's scholarly work includes a book *Graphic Representation of Models of Linguistic Theory* and more than a dozen articles on language and style. Her fiction (which has won two national awards) and her poetry have appeared in the *Southern Review*, *Kansas Quarterly*, the *Chicago Tribune*, and elsewhere. Harleman has lived and worked in the Soviet Union. She has held Guggenheim and Fulbright fellowships and is currently a visiting scholar in the Program in American Civilization at Brown University.

Preface

By all the usual standards of belles lettres, Ian Fleming was a mediocre writer. His characters were improbable and often poorly realized. His plots—they have been called "science fictions"—were unrealistic and seldom credible either within individual episodes or throughout the entire economy of the narrative. His hero lived and worked in a world of cosmic evil confronted by villains who were already several decades out of fashion, if that fashion is to be defined by the work of Fleming's contemporaries. The whole enterprise of his writing was preposterous, ludicrous, and not to be taken at all seriously. And yet the character of James Bond survives when many of his fictional superiors—Alec Leamas, Harry Palmer, Quiller, Boysie Oakes—have faded. James Bond, agent "007," has become for the Western world the epitome of the resourceful and skillful secret agent, a hero of our times.

All of Fleming's James Bond novels have been made into films; the hero's new adventures (under new authorship) continue to be filmed even after the death of his creator. While the influence of Sean Connery was tremendous in shaping the public's perception of Bond's personality, Fleming's character has outlived Connery and Roger Moore, and will outlast Timothy Dalton, the current Bond, and other successors. Connery's assertions that he will not make any more James Bond films always arouse (regretful) public comment and speculation in the media about his successors—and their relative merits—always makes good copy. Even magazine articles about "Bond's girls" attest to the "reality" in the public's mind of the entire espionage good-and-evil world that Fleming has created.

Much has been written about James Bond, during Fleming's life and for several years after, nearly all of it emotionally charged, and a good deal of it rancorous. Some books list Bond's buying habits, and others analyze his sexual preferences. The personality of this fictional secret agent—and not a brilliantly drawn one at that—has impressed itself deeply in our consciousness. Fleming's biographer, John Pearson, has written a "life" of Naval Commander James Bond as though he were real, playfully suggesting that he had been fictionalized in order to conceal the secret nature of his exploits.

In discussing his motivations for writing *The Human Factor* (published in 1978, fourteen years after Fleming's death), Graham Greene wrote that he wanted to "write a novel of espionage free from the conventional violence, which has not, in spite of James Bond, been a feature of the British Secret Service." Bond has been on the minds of real agents; a friend of Sir William Stephenson (the man called "Intrepid") remarked that his wife's funeral was "straight out of James Bond"— referring to the tight-lipped self-control of the mourners and the simplicity of the service; not at all like the Bond that Ian Fleming had created. Real-life spy (and traitor) Kim Philby remembered a World War II Secret Intelligence Service (SIS) discussion that considered alternate ways of moving against the Germans lodged clandestinely in Spain. A diplomatic solution was finally chosen, because no one "on our side would really welcome a James Bond–like free-for-all." And Sidney Reilly's biographer, Robin Bruce Lockhart, wishing to dramatize his subject's accomplishments to an audience largely innocent of the man (the book was written before the release of the British television production, *Reilly: Ace of Spies*), recalls congratulating Ian Fleming after the publication of his first James Bond novel: "James Bond is just a piece of nonsense I dreamed up," his creator demurred, "he's not a Sidney Reilly, you know!" (Lockhart, p. 11).

Fleming, through his Intelligence Service contacts—he was assistant to the director of Naval Intelligence during World War II and knew many people in the spy community—was in an ideal position to hear tales of the life and exploits of Sidney Reilly. And he would also have heard stories of other spies. Fleming knew of the officially sanctioned clandestine assassination of the British seaman who informed the Germans of Allied convoy movements. On assignment in New York with Stephenson's British Security Coordination (BSC) group, he knew of the break-in of the Japanese consultate to steal codebooks. Fleming went to the SIS's training "Camp X" in Canada and himself took a course in underwater demolition, though he failed an exercise in "disposing of a tail." He was with Stephenson when the scheme was hatched to interdict the gold reserves of the Vichy government on Martinique (rather than stealing it), neutralizing its use to the French, making it available to finance BSC operations. Though this real-life scheme never fully materialized, it did inspire *Goldfinger*, which we now consider a thrilling but implausible adventure.

Fleming lived in a time, as we now still do, in which the spy or secret agent fulfilled several deeply felt needs of the general public. The spy subverts bureaucratic society, with its walls, its compartmentalizations, its unwieldly and complex organizations in which a member may not know what his fellow workers are doing and how their contributions complement or conflict with his own work. To a certain extent the espionage apparatus is much like such a society in miniature; the spy's mission takes him into the enemy's bureaucracy, and his invisibility enables him to penetrate those walls, to infiltrate those departments and compartments, and to see what is happening there, to understand how it all fits together.

All the while the spy remains invisible himself; not physically, of course, but through the use of disguises, aliases, manufactured identities. His invisibility enables him to move freely through this hostile environment, seeing everything but not being seen himself, giving him a license that none of his fellow citizens possesses. Agent "007" has a license to kill; in effect, he has been given a license to write his own laws. Trained to deceive and to dissemble, even to kill perhaps, the spy, who is alone and vulnerable and is armed only with his wits and what he can carry on his person, needs invisibility for his protection.

Fleming saw how the vocation of the secret agent would appeal to his contemporaries, how it was an ideal medium for their collective projections. He also felt that our age needed and would admire a genuine hero. Therefore, he created a hero who was much more than just a secret agent, appealing as that role alone might be. In making James Bond, he remade an adventurer of the old mold, a swashbuckler from an older time, a hero who was always equal to whatever task the forces of evil pitted against him. No matter how insidious, how clever, how technologically sophisticated, how wealthy and resourceful, or how well supported and supplied the adversary, Bond would win because of his skills, his courage, his daring, and because he was always fighting on the side of right. Bond is a morally upright Sidney Reilly, a fighter for just causes, a protector of English capitalist Christendom in a world swarming with seemingly unconquerable enemies.

Ian Fleming, who will never be on anyone's all-time distinguished authors list, was able to perceive this ethos among his contemporaries where others had failed. He wrote more than a dozen novels, often despised by literary critics, touching upon these popular and penetrating themes; and he sold millions of them worldwide. Movies based on his fiction have made many millions more aware of, and respectful of, the character of James Bond, ace of secret agents. What makes popular books popular? What was Fleming's formula for literary success? How does the mediocre writer create characters who live on for decades? For more important reasons than the joke about what he did on his way to the bank, Ian Fleming deserves our attention. This book gives it to him.

We had other reasons for writing his book. Much information about Fleming's life has come to light since John Pearson's excellent biography, *The Life of Ian Fleming*, was published in 1966, only two years after Fleming's death—especially through the letters of Ann Fleming, edited by Mark Amory. And we have had more time to evaluate Fleming's writing without the passions (on both sides) that characterized judgments on him while he lived. Everyone acknowledged the Bond "phenomenon," even his most hostile critics; indeed, his enormous popularity was the source of their anger. Enough time has now passed to enable us to approach him dispassionately and to place him with calm deliberation within the context of his contemporaries, of genre writers particularly, and within the society that had so great a fascination for his writing.

We also find that Fleming is worth studying because very few writers have created a fictional character who is so much their author's doppelganger. James Bond is as close a projection of his author's psyche as is any major character of fiction we know of. There is a lesson here for the psychologist of literature. We believe that one of Fleming's most interesting literary contributions is the way in which he symbolized, in the fiction of the Bond cycle, his inner struggles to overcome a desperately unhappy early life, to break through the restraints of family and social class to maturity. For these reasons also we feel that the life and works of Ian Fleming deserve another look.

We are indebted to Pearson's *The Life of Ian Fleming*, with which all biographical work on Fleming must begin. In the composition of our book, Dr. Janet Yanos has been especially helpful in sharing her insights into Fleming's psychological life. Professor John Cawelti has given us many ideas on the Bond novels, and when we have disagreed with him we realize that it is at our risk. And we wish also to thank two authorities on the British Secret Service, Donald MacCormick and Nigel West, for taking the time to correspond with us—about Fleming and his work.

Bruce A. Rosenberg

Brown University

Ann H. Stewart

Brown University

Chronology

1908   Ian Lancaster Fleming born 8 May.

1917   Father, Valentine Fleming, killed in action in France.

1921   Ian sent to Eton.

1926   Enrolled at Sandhurst, England.

1927   Sent to private tutor at Kitzbuhel.

1933   Becomes Reuters correspondent for Moscow spy trial.

1939   Recruited by Naval Intelligence to be assistant to the director of Naval Intelligence.

1941   On special mission to Washington.

1945   Discharged by Navy; becomes Foreign Manager of Kemsley newspapers.

1952   Marries Ann (Charteris) Fleming.

1953   Publication of *Casino Royale*.

1954   *Live and Let Die*.

1955   *Moonraker*.

1956   *Diamonds Are Forever*.

1957   *From Russia, with Love*.

1958   *Doctor No*.

1959   *Goldfinger*; *For Your Eyes Only*.

1961   *Thunderball*.

1962   *The Spy Who Loved Me*; *Octopussy*; the film *Dr. No* produced.

1963   *On Her Majesty's Secret Service*.

1964   *You Only Live Twice*; *Thrilling Cities* published in book form; Ian Fleming dies of fatal heart attack while at Royal St. George's golf club.

1965   *The Man with the Golden Gun*.

Chapter One

The Making of
James Bond's Reputation

Few aspects of Ian Fleming's life suggested that he would one day become a famous writer, or that he would eventually create a character of lasting, international renown. He was a second son, and a great deal of his energies were spent trying to outdo his older brother Peter, who became well-known in certain circles mainly because of several books he published on his travels, often to exotic places. Ian, by contrast, was an outstanding track star while at Eton, but his stay there was cut short when some "trouble" with girls and his possession of a motorcar brought about their parting of the ways. His mother immediately sent him to Sandhurst. He lasted only a year there (1927), leaving full of hostility and resentment against the school.

His widowed mother next sent him to be tutored by Forbes Dennis and his wife, novelist Phyllis Bottome, at Tennerhof, a new and experimental school in Kitzbuhel, Switzerland, where some remembered him as arrogant, prickly, and in general difficult, while others recalled a charming, handsome, witty, and lively young aristocrat (Pearson, p. 34). While he was on the Continent, under the benign influence of Dennis's theories of education, he grew intellectually. He became interested in reading and he gained self-confidence, though modestly. He tinkered with writing fiction. When he was nineteen he wrote a story later remembered by Bottome, and he was full of fanciful and imaginative accounts of his life, often made up on the spot, which he told to everyone at the school.

His behavior at Tennerhof was in the mold of a Byronic image, a role that was to characterize his life-style for the rest of his years. As at Eton and Sandhurst, he had many girlfriends; they remembered the handsome Englishman who invented adventurous plots in which to recast his everyday life. At the same time his desire for rich food and expensive automobiles was beginning to grow. Yet he also punished himself with a strong puritan streak. The psyche of Ian Fleming was a

1

battlefield. License and puritanical restraint—id and superego—were constantly at war within him. One urge would control him for a time, only to be counterattacked in the next instant by its opposite.

In 1931 Fleming failed the British Diplomatic Service examination, getting his lowest marks, ironically, in the essay section. Perhaps he had too much imagination for his prospective Diplomatic Service employers, for despite the test results, he was an able writer. He came to the attention of Reuters, which sent him to Moscow in 1931 to cover the trial of several British engineers accused of spying. He was an inventive reporter, particularly in the way he managed to get his story on the wire to London first, outsmarting several older and more experienced hands. Significantly, his accounts were imaginative and fanciful, and he frequently made events appear more dramatic than they were in reality. It was on this trip to Moscow, a former friend of his had told us, that Fleming probably heard stories about the famous British secret agent, Sidney Reilly, thought to have been killed in Russia only a few years before. Reporting on an actual trial and listening to adventure stories about the legendary Reilly, the young novelist was learning his craft.

Sefton Delmer, who would later become his colleague in British Intelligence, remembers traveling in Russia with fellow reporter Ian Fleming. They were leaving Moscow on the Warsaw Express, Delmer with prepared notes he had written for a series of articles on life in the Soviet Union. Censorship had been so intense, he relates, that he had been forced to save much of what he had intended to write for the border-crossing. As they approached the frontier, he memorized his notes, tore them up, and threw them away. Fleming teased him mockingly: "Why don't you swallow them? That is what all the best spies do."

They were reporters, not spies—although Fleming's mission in Moscow was not uncomplicated. If Delmer has reported Fleming's remark accurately, it displays a revealing slip. Nevertheless, when they reached the Polish frontier their luggage was searched by the border guards; Delmer's perfunctorily, Fleming's in great detail. Did the guards know something? Finally, they made their big discovery: a carton of contraceptives made of Russian synthetic latex which Fleming was carrying back to London to be chemically analyzed. Delmer remarks innocently that "the future creator of James Bond was already taking an interest in intelligence matters." Without any trace of irony, the Russian guards held each "sample" to the light and examined it. Delmer whispered, "You should have swallowed them" (1961, pp. 390–91).

Was Fleming's job in Moscow simply that of reporter, or were there other aspects to it as well? England's Secret Intelligence Service (SIS) had frequently used reporters for confidential missions (Knightley, p. 91). Their occupation made them ideal agents: they traveled widely and were politically knowledgeable, and their profession had trained them to gather and assess information. In the 1920s SIS had employed the *Times* correspondent to Rome; subsequently, writers for the *Manchester Guardian,* the *Daily Express,* and the *Daily Mirror* had worked for them.

Upon his demobilization from the Navy in 1945, Fleming had another go at journalism. Before the war he had achieved only one article with a byline, in the *Daily Express* in 1933. But he was nothing if not well-connected, a fact that counted for much in certain spheres of English society, and those connections would land him on his feet. In 1947 he wrote an essay on Jamaica for friend Cyril Connolly's magazine, *Horizon.* The inevitable happened, and he began working for Lord Kemsley's media empire as foreign manager for the Kemsley group. Richard Deacon, who worked for Fleming as his Commonwealth correspondent in London and later as assistant foreign manager, has reminded us (personal correspondence) that in those days Fleming was in charge of the foreign department of all of the Kemsley newspapers— not only the *Sunday Times,* but three other national Sunday papers and "countless" provincial daily and evening papers as well. According to John Pearson, Fleming's biographer and himself a journalist for the Kemsley chain, "for someone with so little experience of journalism it was one of the sleekest appointments of the year" (p. 153). Fleming shortly set about building up one of the most considerable organizations in the news business, the Mercury service. But he was neither a frugal nor a careful manager, perhaps having been spoiled by habits he had acquired during the war at the Admiralty, and he really did not have a reporter's sense of what was newsworthy.

In the late 1940s the Mercury service began to founder. Higher positions within Kemsley's empire became available, but Fleming was consistently by-passed. By 1950 he realized that the great career that he had imagined for himself in journalism was through. As well—or maybe as a result—he was unhappy in his work. And at forty he had to face the unpleasant fact that he was, after all, a son disinherited by

English inheritance law (even though his grandfather was a millionaire investment banker—he died in 1933). His health and his career (such as it was) began to slide. The future was looking grim indeed.

In 1952 Fleming married Ann Charteris—recently divorced from Esmond, the second Viscount Rothermere—with whom he had been having an affair. It was a turbulent relationship. She had written to him two years earlier that she found him "a selfish thoughtless bastard" (Amory, p. 79). They loved each other ferociously at first, but eventually they drifted apart—physically, because his writing assignments carried him around the world while she was continually drawn back to her society friends in and near London; and emotionally, because each had a passionate dislike for the other's life-style.

Ann's two previous husbands had complained about her friends. Ian was no different. Indeed, it is doubtful if any of Ann's friends were disliked by either previous husband as intensely as they were by Fleming. They in turn derided his books, and as his success grew, so did their mockery (Amory, p. 115). Ann thought him "much calmer" when they were alone together and observed that he was "only going mad" when he saw her relations and friends (Amory, p. 333). In various letters to her friends, she complained about Ian's "notorious tact," his hammering away at his "pornography," his rudeness and his irrational outbursts (Amory, pp. 136, 169, 221–22). She found it "unwise" ever to contradict him (Amory, p. 262). In letters to close friends, she at first referred to her husband as the "commander" (as he was widely known to Jamaican natives), but later called him "Thunderbird" (presumably for the car he bought with his first large royalty check), or "Thunderball," or "the Beatle" (who were also popular at the time and, Ann felt, equally mindless). Sometimes it was "Thunderbeatle" or simply "TB."

After a vacation to Kitzbuhel—nostalgic for Ian, of course—Ann, in a letter to Evelyn Waugh (4 January 1961; Amory, p. 277), called him the "Kitzbuhel Casanova." The vacation would have been a disaster for him, she thought, but for a fourteen-year-old German girl named Lilo ("hun for Lolita?" she wondered), who "fastens his skis and collects him from snowdrifts." He was adversely affected by the altitude, and had to be propped up with pillows at night because of his panting.

In one of Fleming's persistent waking dreams, he had vowed that he would one day write the world's greatest adventure story. It was one of the more revealing fantasies of his young adulthood, maybe even of his early middle age. He wrote *Casino Royale* and showed it to his friend William Plomer (who had connections at Jonathan Cape, Publishers), who liked it. The editors at Cape also liked it. They published it, and Ian Fleming was on his way. James Bond was on his way, too, and this new master spy's professional life and reputation started to become indelibly imprinted on the public's mind.

"James Bond" was the name of a real ornithologist; Fleming found it on the cover of his copy of the *Birds of the West Indies* in 1952. He said that he wanted the most ordinary and undistinguished of names for his hero, and "James Bond" was perfect. Bond the ornithologist was later invited to visit with Fleming and was greatly amused by the story.

During the war Fleming's travels had taken him to Jamaica, and he had fallen in love with the place; he bought a beach house on a comfortable lot (later named "Goldeneye") and lived there for two months each year. The working conditions were ideal for him at Goldeneye; he wrote for three hours in the morning, took a siesta in the afternoon, rose again at five to edit what he had typed, and began drinking at 6:30. He ground out two thousand words a day—for *Casino Royale,* sixty-two thousand in all. Two-and-a-half months later—18 March 1952—*Casino Royale* was completed, seemingly effortlessly to casual observers. It was written at Ann's suggestion, to ward off boredom; as he facetiously put it, to take his mind "off the shock of getting married at the age of forty three" (Pearson, pp. 190–91).

Bond was an unlikely hero/adventurer/spy. Fleming never thought much of him—and at first not much about him. The whole enterprise was to be that of the effortless Etonian who above all must not appear to have worked very hard. Hard work on such a plebian production was definitely infra dig. Fleming did not work long—two months at a time was about all the working space he could afford. But when he was writing he did put a lot of effort into it. Yet the public stance was paramount; in a letter to Plomer, Fleming once referred to Bond as "that cardboard booby." He once claimed that in *Casino Royale* the dialogue, much of the description, and the main characters are "dreadfully banal" (Pearson, p. 206).

Success was not immediate, as we shall see, either for *Casino Royale* or for the first few books that followed at the quick pace of about one a year. But when fortune finally smiled on him, it was from ear to ear. Critic LeRoy Panek thought that Fleming's success was largely "a historical accident" that made a public figure of a "muddled hero created by a third-rate hack" (Panek, p. 219). Fleming was only made famous, according to this critic, by the movies and the appearance of a Bond novel on President Kennedy's "Favorite List." Whatever the relation of this list to Kennedy's actual tastes—it has been suggested that the president merely wanted to include some popular fare on the list, so as to appear to be just plain folks at heart—Ann did write to friend Clarissa Avon (16 February 1964; Amory, p. 336) that Bobby Kennedy was "obsessed" by Ian's books.

James Bond was so famous and so frequently discussed that to some people he became real. William Stevenson, author of *A Man Called Intrepid,* recalls the man who insisted that Bond really lived but had been fictionalized by Fleming and others in order to deceive his enemies. The "alleged Bond" was "unmasked" in Bermuda's Hamilton Princess Hotel (the city's oldest and poshest) where he was known to have occupied a suite belonging to Sir William Stephenson. As proof, the unmasker cited the hotel's "Gazebo Bar," which has a large fish tank much like the glass shark tank in *Doctor No.*

The print run for the first edition of *Casino Royale* was a modest 4,750. Subsequent editions added to that number, but not impressively until after the movie version was released. The first three American publishers to consider the book—Doubleday, Norton, and Knopf—turned it down. For *Live and Let Die,* Fleming began to recast three newspaper articles he had written about Cousteau's underwater explorations for sunken treasure. While he was working on this material, MacMillan bought the rights to *Casino Royale.*

Working again for just two months a year at Goldeneye, Fleming finished *Moonraker* in June 1954, commenting to friends that "it isn't much of a book, but it should make a good film" (Pearson, p. 249). His friend Philip Brownrigg, who worked for de Beers, South African diamond miners and merchants, gave Fleming a great deal of information about the precious gem business, used in *Diamonds Are Forever.* When that book was finished, in March 1955, Fleming thought it better than *Moonraker,* though he never told friends why.

Ann wrote in 1956 that his new book (*Diamonds are Forever*) was "Ian's new horror comic" (Amory, p. 181). She did not understand the popular success of his nonfiction essays, *Thrilling Cities,* but she felt that they needed the money, so she was not going to question the public's taste too closely (Amory, p. 268). In 1960 she could write to Evelyn Waugh that Ian's only happiness lay in "pink gin, golf clubs, and men" (Amory, p. 270). To Ian (in March [?] 1962) she wrote, "if you were well and we were both younger our marriage would be over . . . your personality has changed greatly with success, Bond, and bad health—this is a *general* opinion" (Amory, p. 302). He replied that all he had ever gotten from her was complaints and that all that had gone wrong "has been laid at my door" (Amory, p. 303).

Even with this literary production and with American movie makers beginning to take an interest, James Bond had yet to become a household word. The American edition of *Live and Let Die* sold only 5,000 copies in 1955, and though *Casino Royale* was filmed, it was almost at once shelved. Fleming sold the rights to it, and with the money bought a Thunderbird. Ann found it "above our price bracket and below our age range" (Pearson, p. 258). But it was a piece of Ian's dream.

Fleming was as determined as he was prolific. Disappointed that his adventure stories were not selling as widely as he wanted, he urged many of his friends and connections to promote the books. Eventually his writing caught on. It was characteristic of this complex man that he wanted his novels to look as though they had been casually and effortlessly dashed off by a talented dilettante, but actually Fleming wanted them to sell, wanted the success and the notoriety they would bring him, and wanted the money from the royalties.

And he wanted these things right away. In 1957, to the chagrin of his friends, he accepted an offer by an American publisher to have James Bond's adventures put into a comic strip. Desperate for cash, he sold the movie rights to *Casino Royale* to Gregory Ratoff in 1954 for a paltry $6,000. The book was later sold again (to Charles Feldman) as a satire, and in that form was produced (Rubin, p. 2). Beginning *Doctor No,* Fleming vowed to an American editor, Al Hart, that he was going to write the "same book over and over again" (Pearson, p. 286), for the sake of simplicity, for ease of creation, and adherence to a proven formula. And, to his critics' disgust but his readers' delight, he did. *Goldfinger* followed easily and formulaically in 1957.

The JFK "endorsement" in a *Life* magazine article (17 March 1961) listing *From Russia with Love* among his ten favorite books started Fleming's ball rolling. Kennedy may or may not have been a James Bond fan; whatever JFK's motivation, news of the "endorsement" was public property. In August 1961 Hollywood producers Harry Saltzman and Albert Broccoli took options on all the Bond novels. Fleming was to get $100,000 and five percent of the producer's profit for each of them (Rubin, p. 9).

Other factors helped. The 1950s were the right time for the intro-duction of a spy adventurer who, loyal and patriotic, would do his able best to right the vertiginous plight of the world. There was a spate of spy exposés in the Western press. In England and the United States the public's awareness of espionage, of covert cold war activities, of international intrigue, was raised. In 1956 the Hungarians rebelled and were violently subdued by Russian troops, and in 1961 the East Germans raised a wall across the boundary line in Berlin, to "keep out Western spies." In 1961 an astonished world watched the aborted Bay of Pigs invasion; in 1962 the Cuban missile crisis occurred. Maclean and Burgess disappeared and shortly after turned up at a Moscow press conference. Later, Kim Philby, their associate and a British Intelligence officer, escaped to Russia and was revealed to have been a KGB officer all along. In the United States Senator Joseph McCarthy found traitors and spies everywhere. There was Alger Hiss in particular—a former official in the State Department—and the Rosenbergs, executed for passing atomic secrets to the Russians. The time was right for the spy-as-hero.

Here is the turning point in Fleming's life. From 1960 to 1962 he made £250,000 on book royalties; but after 1962, when *Doctor No* was filmed, money came to him by the carload. *From Russia, with Love* was produced the next year, *Goldfinger* in 1964, *Thunderball* (which even-tually grossed $52 million) in 1965, and on and on. Only one Bond novel, *The Man with the Golden Gun,* failed to sell two million copies (Van Dover, p. 5); that was Fleming's last book, and by general con-sensus his poorest. The movie version of *From Russia, with Love* grossed $460,186 in its first week in New York alone (Tornabuoni, quoted in Eco, p. 19). And as the movies multiplied Bond's popularity, book sales got a second wind. From June through August 1964, for in-stance, more than 480,000 James Bond novels were sold in French translation alone; by 1965 that figure had surpassed two million (Tor-nabuoni, quoted in Eco, pp. 19–20).

It is an ironic comment on Fleming's fame that Saltzman and Broc-coli always hired screenwriters (usually Richard Maibaum and Tom Mankiewicz, occasionally Joanna Harwood, once Roald Dahl) to do major rewrites on the original novels. In the end it was the movies—on which James Bond's fame largely rests—that created the fame of their hero/secret agent. Fleming had little to do with that. For their $100,000 a film, Saltzman and Broccoli bought a title, a few characters, and an occasional exotic setting. The plots, the witty dialogues, the gimmickry, the very character of James Bond, all were made in England's Pinewood Studios and Hollywood. The Bond movies made an international star out of a one-time coffin polisher and dancer in *South Pacific* (Tornabuoni, quoted in Eco, p. 16) named Sean Connery. Ironically, Fleming is said to have been dissatisfied with Connery—who became James Bond for many millions of moviegoers—because he was not what he had in mind.

Though he once deprecated his notoriety with the comment that "you've no idea how bored one gets with the whole silly business" (Pearson, p. 342), Fleming loved it. To celebrate that filming of *From Russia, with Love,* for instance, he flew to Paris to buy £500 worth of Beluga caviar and hustled back to London with it for an unforgettable party. He had had the first of his serious heart attacks earlier that April (1961), but now he was finally earning the amounts of money he had always wanted.

In June 1964 Ann wrote to Evelyn Waugh that Ian had by that time won nine "Pan Book Oscars," one for each book which had sold more than one million copies (Pan was Fleming's paperback publisher in England). She was astonished and delighted. Snide about the entire enterprise, she was at the same time proud of Ian's accomplishments. She was worried about Ian's failing health and his refusal to make any accommodation to his situation. In only two months—though she of course could not know this—the end would come for him.

His first serious heart attack, on 12 April 1961, had, not surprisingly, a traumatic effect. He was fifty-three at the time. Several more attacks struck him during the next several years, a period during which his letters but especially his conversations were morbid and fatalistic. He cut down on his drinking and smoking only slightly, but this concession to fate was enacted with bitterness. He was never peacefully resigned to his impending death. The final attack struck him after attending a golf club committee meeting at the Royal St. Georges' (the original for "St. Mark's" club set in *Goldfinger*), on 11 August 1964. He was taken to a local hospital, where he died at approximately 1:00 a.m. the following morning.

At Fleming's death, the Bond novels had sold more than forty mil-

lion copies, and James Bond was an international cult figure. Ian had
outshone his brother and his grandfather in the world's marketplace,
though they probably would not have recognized his triumph. Ironically, Ian Fleming himself, with a profound inner sadness, might well
have agreed with them.

Chapter Two
Ian Fleming:
A Personality Profile

The second son of a wealthy, socially prominent Scottish family, Fleming was psychologically a classic case. His investment banker grandfather Robert, who died in 1933, was a self-made millionaire. One of his many interests was the Anglo-Persian Oil Co. Ian's mother, Evelyn St. Croix Rose, claimed among her ancestors Sir Richard Quain, editor of the *Dictionary of Medicine,* and (more remotely) John of Gaunt. Ian Lancaster Fleming's middle name honors the connection with Gaunt. Ian's father, Valentine Fleming, invested a large portion of his inheritance in a several-hundred-acre estate. Such were the surroundings into which, on 28 May 1908, Ian Lancaster was born: wealth, dynastic land holdings, a listing in *Burke's Landed Gentry.* It was a life-style to which he would become addicted. A friend of his maturity, Ernest Cuneo, has written that "Fleming was really quite simple to understand, but only within the complex class structure of the British civilization into the upper stratum of which he was born" (Benson, p. xi).

Ian was nearly nine years old when his father was killed while in action in Picardy, on 20 May 1917. It was a catastrophe for the family, of course, but not unnoticed by the nation at large. The event was notable enough for the London *Times* to print an obituary written by Winston Churchill, a fellow Conservative M.P. For Ian, this death was to have effects more lasting than the expected ones. The dead, hallowed father became an ideal his widow held up to her four sons. The halo around his memory, lovingly constructed by Evelyn, meant that Valentine became a sacred model that Ian could not possibly equal, much less surpass. According to Adlerian psychology, the mother usually favors the first born—in this case Peter Fleming. According to Adlerian theory, the father then acts as a counterbalance by giving preference to the younger child. Since Ian's father was not available to him when he was passing through adolescence, he missed out on nearly all parental affection and encouragement, which would have been lavished instead on Peter.

Under the English law of primogeniture, the eldest son inherits everything. The idea, theoretically, is to preserve the family's capital while the disinherited share vicariously in the benefits, striving all the while to establish their own fortunes. In the Fleming family this unitary inheritance seemed to include parental affections and talent as well. Peter, the favored one, published first, and acquired a certain fame for several travel books: *Brazilian Adventure, News from Tartary, The Siege at Peking, Bayonets to Lhasa, The Fate of Admiral Kolchak,* amongst others. Mark Amory, the editor of Ann Fleming's letters, has described Peter as among the most promising young men in the country, one "on whom the elder generation beamed approval." A blurb accompanying Ian's first novel, *Casino Royale,* described him—much to Ian's distress—as the brother of Peter Fleming. Ian was competitive—or perhaps became competitive in order to survive within the social context of his immediate family—but he was destined always to finish second to "this paragon"; there was little alternative, Amory contends, to his becoming the family's black sheep (p. 35). The contrast between the brothers was exacerbated by Peter's impressive scholastic success at Eton: admired and envied, he won all the prizes (Pearson, pp. 26–27). So the future creator of James Bond spent his adolescent energies trying to outdo his brother and failing the task.

Like many young men of his class, Ian was sent to Eton, a prestigious school for the sons of the social elite. Ian was not a distinguished scholar at Eton, nor did he impress anyone with his writing ability. Before his class graduated, he was forced to withdraw after violating at least two school rules, one having to do with girls and the other with his ownership of a car.

Although Ian Fleming did not suffer an inordinate number of failures in his life, he strove never to admit to any. Saving face was vital to him, even if it meant covering up his flaws to close friends. In his introduction to *The James Bond Bedside Companion,* Ernest Cuneo writes:

I was amazed to learn that Fleming had not graduated from either Eton or Sandhurst, which he certainly permitted and even encouraged me to believe. In fact, he even told me that on graduation from Sandhurst, he had selected the Black Watch as his regiment. I was also under the impression he left the foreign service for journalism.

Actually, he had not; he never belonged to it. (Benson, p. xii)

Much of the mature Fleming's character is revealed through his friend's anecdote. He was very much concerned with appearances, but only of a certain kind; though actually a rebel against the life that was expected of him—especially as dictated by his mother—in later years he wanted it thought that he had actually done the "right" things, gone to the "right" schools, associated with the "right" people—in other words, that he had properly prepared himself for a conventional upper-class life. That established, he could afford to be casual about his accomplishments—at Eton, at Sandhurst, and so forth. But before one can be cavalier about Eton, one has to have graduated from the school. In Ian Fleming's case, the attitude was a pose adopted after the fact—or nonfact.

It was after the Sandhurst failure that Ian's mother sent him to be privately tutored by Forbes Dennis at Tennerhof in Kitzbuhel, Switzerland. Dennis's first impression of the younger Fleming—he met Peter as well—was of a young Englishman, "very good-looking, very arrogant, very Etonian and very prickly" (Pearson, p. 34). The Swiss setting was idyllic, and the young Scotsman responded with considerable charm (of which he was to be capable throughout his life) as well as arrogant petulance. Under the benign influence of Phyllis Bottome, who was an ardent admirer of Alfred Adler, whose system she cherished and whose biographer she became, Ian became interested in psychology. He even engaged in a brief correspondence with the Swiss psychologist Carl Jung. But his interest in the formal aspects of psychology was not a lasting one. He also met Einstein briefly, was enormously impressed, and remembered the meeting long afterwards.

But Fleming was the classic gentleman dilettante. (In his mature years he only sought the company of those he considered "fine people" [Benson, p. 43] and would not be bothered by those who bored him; one of his greatest stated fears throughout his life was of being bored.) He became interested in books under the encouragement of Dennis—though he also began collecting various oddities, in his own variant of souvenir-hoarding. In 1935 he commissioned Percy Muir to begin a collection of books, whose only criterion was that they be "milestones of human progress." Friend Evelyn Waugh, enthusiastic about the project, later suggested that it ought to include works on religion. Characteristically, Fleming read hardly any of them; for him, it was enough just to own such a collection, to have the appearance of a scholarly bibliophile. Four years later, in 1939, he claimed the collection was worth around £100,000 (Pearson, pp. 78–79).

Forbes was successful in restoring Ian's confidence in himself and in making at least a minimal scholar of him. Bottome liberated his creative faculties, and he dabbled in writing. She met regularly with the students and encouraged them to construct truthful stories about their lives as they had lived them, and also to invent narratives. At nineteen Ian invented a story about a minor nobleman who raped an unprotesting virgin (inspired by Thomas Hardy?) and acquired leprosy from her (Pearson, pp. 39–40) and a short story, "Death on Two Occasions," certainly inspired by Bottome. She had herself written a spy novel, *The Lifeline* (1946), but there is no evidence that Ian got the idea for espionage fiction from her. Friends at Tennerhof later remembered his imaginative powers and his invented (and usually adventurous) "plots" for the events of his everyday life (Pearson, pp. 44–45). This imaginative view of life would stay with him.

Another pattern set in those days was that of his relations with women. He is remembered at Tennerhof as the "high romantic exile" (Pearson, p. 42)—"an amorist by nature," as a Swiss acquaintance put it (Pearson, p. 43). His succession of Swiss girlfriends all clearly remember the charming, handsome Englishman. He pouted and sulked a great deal, perfecting his Byronic image. The "good things" in life were irresistible to him—but he usually felt guilty when he got them. A friend recalled to Fleming's biographer John Pearson that Ian longed for women, rich foods, and expensive cars, but that he punished himself for getting them (p. 46).

While Fleming was the brooding Byronic melancholic at Tennerhof, his persona was entirely different in town: charming, cheerful, full of fun and wit. Dennis arranged for Ian to study at the University of Munich (although there is no evidence that he ever attended a lecture there), and a year later he studied at the University of Geneva. The arrangements were informal: he was not enrolled as a regular degree candidate, and he lived with private families in each town. While studying in Geneva he became interested in one young woman in particular, the daughter of a well-to-do Geneva landowner. They became informally engaged, but when Ian brought his sweetheart home to mother for approval, Evelyn was not pleased. She was a loving mother when her children were obedient, but she could be severe when crossed. Ian feared her enough not to cross her. The engagement was broken—shattered was more like it. It was to have a lasting effect on his life, particularly in the way he allowed himself to respond to women. Shy by inclination, Fleming had now seen a relationship he held dear dismantled by others. He determined never to make emotional attachments that others could destroy; he would never again be vulnerable. He vowed to "take what I want" from women, "without any scruples at all" (Pearson, p. 57). That attitude would prevail for the rest of his life.

Maintaining the attitude of a disinterested dilettante was important to Fleming, as it was to many of his social class. The idea was to do a number of things well—especially the "right" things—but never to appear as though much preparation or practice had been necessary. Nothing was to be taken too seriously or too strenuously. Joan Rockwell has named the syndrome "ritual frivolity," an expression of the uppermost myth of British aristocracy: the display of effortless superiority. The elite can do everything well, and they can do it with ease, without practice, while the lower orders must work at their tasks arduously and still the results of their efforts are bound to be inferior. At Eton Ian's excellence in track, especially at the intermediate distances, was intended to be thought of simply as something he did well, naturally, and effortlessly; gentlemen did not labor greatly for such events, and they never, ever perspired. Schoolday photographs show Ian (and his classmates, to be sure) participating in track events in what look like street clothes; certainly they are all very casually attired for such strenuous activities. As a friend of his mature years, Yvar Bryce, put it, Ian never took himself "too seriously" (p. 102).

He had the carriage and attitude of a young man who did not train himself for his track competitions, but he did seem to have trained himself never to become deeply involved with the men and women of his world. If they could not immediately gratify him or further his ambitions in some way, he did not seem to have been interested in them. Most of the people who met him more or less casually, never got to know him very well, thought him aloof and disinterested; others occasionally saw an entirely different face: when he wanted to, he could be enormously charming. His mother thought that he would make an excellent diplomat, and she responded warmly to Forbes Dennis's suggestion that Ian prepare for the foreign service exam. He seems to have worked seriously on the project, but he nevertheless failed the exam, and when he learned the results of the test he was profoundly dejected. He finished twenty-fifth out of sixty-two (Pearson, 54). Only the first five candidates received appointments; so in later years Fleming claimed that he had been only one place away from successful placement.

In several ways Fleming could have been the model for what psychologist Karen Horney has termed the "detached personality." Such people, she wrote in *Our Inner Conflicts,* have a neurotic drive not to become dependent on others in any way—a compulsive need for self-sufficiency (p. 75). They are usually reticent, very private personalities (p. 76) who have difficulty with long-term commitments—leases, contracts, marriages—because of the dependent obligations they entail. In the drive for self-sufficiency the detached personality may reject all conventional rules and societal standards (p. 78). The detached person believes that his or her hidden greatness—often concealed or denigrated—should be recognized by others without effort on the subject's part (p. 80). So Fleming—for whom Bond was a "cardboard booby," and who wrote his novels ostensibly to help him get over the shock of getting married so late in life—intensely wanted to be acknowledged by the critics, by intellectuals, by other writers, by the people his wife associated with.

Artists, according to Horney, often adopt the strategy of detachment. Frequently they suffer a kind of numbness as adolescents, their creativity following upon disastrous attempts at closeness (p. 83). Fleming could hardly be better described. Detachment protects one's integrity in a deceitful world, in a world where one may be vulnerable to outside forces, vulnerable to other people. Of course, too much detachment leads to paranoia. But we should also recognize that spies often live in a detached world; John Le Carré has recently stated that a spy novelist is only as good as his paranoia.

Friend Ivar Bryce (p. 39 ff.) remembered with particular vividness an automobile tour of Europe. Ian showed up with an unannounced companion, an attractive American woman named Phyllis. Their itinerary would take them through Germany into Austria. Bryce thought Phyllis was very clever, a rare woman who could match Fleming's banter thrust for thrust. But Ian quickly tired of her, and tried to abandon her in Munich. As he attempted to leave her at curbside, in front of their hotel, she jumped on the runningboard; Fleming then accelerated until she jumped off. He explained to Bryce that "she would madden us with her demands . . . we could have stayed there arguing with her all day." Ian felt that he was perfectly justified in abandoning Phyllis because she could take care of herself in Munich—she had plenty of money and therefore could manage anything.

The pose of the Byronic hero—melancholy, moody, eccentric, easily and frequently bored, given to dramatic moments of despondency and world-weary pessimism—was ideal for the second son of a wealthy family, outshone by an elder brother and repressed by a strong-willed mother. Fleming became a Don Juan, seducing a great variety of young women, dispassionately, resentful of any demands they might make upon him, occasionally ending his affairs with them brusquely and unfeelingly.

He never seemed to outgrow his mother's dominance. In 1963 (Fleming was then in his mid-fifties) his wife, Ann, wrote to Evelyn Waugh (Amory, p. 324) that Ian's mother still treated him as though he were twelve years old. One time he met her in Monte Carlo where he had gone to "collect" her, because she was too old to travel alone. She had it in mind that they would share a sleeper and a picnic dinner, but that scene was avoided. Nevertheless, he was assigned to carry her jewel case and the X-rays of her gall bladder, as well as to oversee the disposition of her fourteen cabin trunks. She had become convinced that she was bankrupt and that her sons were millionaires, and they became the prisoners of this fantasy life, living in constant fear of dis- inheritance. Fleming did not dare to appear wealthy in her presence lest his mother take advantage.

Boredom was even harder than his mother to overcome. And this dread—natural or self-induced—was passed on to James Bond. Early in *Moonraker* (p. 9) we are told that

It was the beginning of a typical routine day for Bond. It was only two or three times a year that an assignment came along requiring his particular abilities. For the rest of the year he had the duties of an easy-going senior civil servant—elastic office hours from around ten to six; lunch, generally in the canteen; evenings spent playing cards in the company of a few close friends, or at Crockford's; or making love, with rather cold passion, to one of three similarly disposed married women; week-ends playing golf for rather high stakes at one of the clubs near London.

Ian's broken engagement—dissolved because of his mother's dis- pleasure—was an event that shaped his later life enormously. It is worth repeating his explicit vow thereafter to "take what I want" from women "without any scruples at all." He would treat women as objects to be used and then discarded. In his own mind he emphasized the pleasure to be derived from them, but until his marriage, at age forty- three, he never became attached to any woman as a human being. Friendship with other men was possible—although he does not seem to have allowed himself to become very close or confiding to any male friend, either: witness Ernest Cuneo's anecdote about having been led to believe that Fleming had graduated from Eton and Sandhurst. But with women, Fleming was especially detached and manipulative.

Before he married, Fleming had many lovers (there is some indication that after marriage he had at least one as well). He was bored by many of the women he seduced almost immediately afterward, and he was elusive with them all. He played the part, his biographer Pearson thought, of the unprincipled seducer (p. 81). Fleming was a womanizer who—and this is common enough—did not really like women. Only men could be intellectual; women were happy animals to be petted, who provided men with sensual pleasures. No sexual relationship was allowed to engage his complete self, not because he could not, but because he *would* not give of himself in any such liaison.

Fleming isolated himself from the society through which he moved. Because he was "fundamentally isolated" as a person (Pearson's phrase, p. 196), as a writer he was never able to create a credible character. Fleming was uninterested in human character (surely a great weakness for a novelist); he lavished his curiosity instead on objects: his interest in automobiles, in what he considered to be fine food, and his detailing of these interests in his novels are well known.

Testimony concerning Fleming's culinary tastes is mixed. Friend Noel Coward thought that the black crabs served in the Fleming house tasted like "cigarette ash out of a pink tin" and that their meals in general at Goldeneye in Jamaica tasted "like armpits" (Pearson, pp. 142, 176.) But that was part of the Coward wit and charm: he also referred to Fleming's Caribbean home as "Goldeneye, nose and throat." The Fleming cuisine was so bad that he crossed himself "before each morsel." His host's sofa was "upholstered with iron shavings"; "All you Flemings," Coward once told him, "revel in discomfort" (Amory, p. 55). John Pearson remarks that "it is hard to think of a single subject on which he [Fleming] was a genuine expert" (p. 210). Fleming's knowledge of food was "erratic," of wine almost "non-existent." Although a good driver, he relied on others for the detailed facts of automotive technology. So, too, says Pearson, with weaponry, gambling, high finance, even on matters concerning the Secret Service. "Only on matters of sex did he rely entirely on his own carefully guarded expertise" (p. 210).

But perhaps the most salient "objects" in Fleming's novels are women. His heroines are also distanced and in important ways depersonalized—they are often the obvious vehicles of their author's sexual fantasies and wishes. Only their exotic names—Vesper, Tiffany, Solitaire, Honeychile, Gala, Pussy, Domino, Kissy, etc.—seem to individualize them. But they appear in consistent, ready compliance with Bond's lusts (except Hugo Drax's administrative assistant, Gala Brand, in *Moonraker,* who is engaged to another man and so informs Bond at the novel's end.) They are nearly all two-dimensional, and all have secondary roles in the novels. Bond and the villain are the only really important characters.

In a 1960 interview Fleming revealingly stated that women were "absolutely filthy" creatures (Pearson, p. 84), that they never washed enough; not even American women, he thought, though that nation's women came closest to his ideal. The rest of the world was at this time complaining of America's overconcern with cleanliness, and American women were usually criticized for being too fastidious about personal hygiene. This feeling—that women were "filthy" creatures who did not bother to wash themselves properly—provided Fleming with his rationale for "using" women (with a cold passion) and for shunning any meaningful relationships with them. Fleming's creation Bond is fastidious; he is continually taking showers—the four (plus one bath) in *Doctor No* are typical.

Turning forty was a trauma for Fleming, more so than for most men. To symbolize his desire for a change of life he decided on his life's costume: a blue polka-dot tie, black moccasins, a dark blue suit. Those sartorial decisions, trivial in themselves, signified the deeper changes he wished to bring about. At age forty he thought of himself as a profoundly disadvantaged, disinherited second son, a man whose life had come to nothing. He quit the Kemsley newspaper chain, for which he had worked for years. His health and his career were slipping away. What to do now? He was smoking seventy cigarettes a day and drinking a quarter of a bottle of gin before he slept.

Then in 1952 he married Ann Charteris. They had been having a jet-set, clandestine romance for more than a year while she was still married to her second husband, Esmond, Lord Rothermere. During the summer of 1951 all of the self-doubts he had been having about his impending marriage, his lack of money, his health, his advancing age, and his life-style surfaced. During all of this Sturm und Drang her divorce proceedings ground inexorably on. Ann was entirely dif-

ferent from the many women he had already slept with; she made no
demands on him (an attitude bound to be successful with Ian), and she
was witty, occasionally even outrageous. And, no doubt most important for Fleming, she was well-connected.

Perhaps their sporadic meetings fueled romantic feelings; since their
marriage was tumultuous, that is easy to guess. In any event, Ann was
unhappy with Esmond, finding him lacking in ambition, stingy, a
man of narrow interests and poor judgment in his appraisals of people,
and boring (Amory, p. 91 ff.). While still married to him she became
pregnant with Ian's child; it died several hours after a premature birth
on 18 July 1948. Early in 1952 she could write to her brother, Hugo
Charteris, that her marriage was "dissolved" (Amory, p. 104). Shortly
after, she married Ian at Goldeneye.

At the very least their marriage was going to be a tempestuous one,
and they both knew it. He relished solitude and his own counsel. She
was most comfortably in her element amidst a swirl of "the rich, powerful and amusing." Mark Amory claims that the phrase "political
hostess" does not really describe her, though she did entertain many of
the most prominent politicians of the day, amongst others. He says
that she was an ideal hostess because she made people wittier and cleverer than they had ever been, wittier and cleverer than they thought
themselves capable of being. Later in her party-giving career, she cul-
tivated the friendship of writers and painters.

In one letter she complains that after dinner they would go out to
the nearby cliffs, and gaze out at the sea, and that Ian would remain
there long after she and their "chaperone" had retired, smoking "and
wallowing in the melancholy" (Amory, p. 61). This moodiness took
place in 1948, with marriage still nearly four years away. When Fleming wanted to decorate Goldeneye, Ann gave the matter some
thought—only to have him disregard all of her advice. She described
herself to him as a "snarky girl accustomed to money"; a year later
(early in 1950) she berated him, not entirely seriously, as "a selfish
thoughtless bastard" (Amory, pp. 78–79).

Still, they claimed that they loved each other. Fleming saw all the
ways in which they were different, but he was in love and did not
think that it would matter. Or more likely, he thought that their love
would overcome all of the differences between them. At the end of
February 1952 he wrote to her brother (and his wife) predicting a
stormy marriage: "china will fly" (Amory, p. 106).

It was Ann who suggested that he take up writing, to ward off boredom. So he sat down at Goldeneye to write his first novel. *Casino Royale* was finished in less than three months, by mid-March 1952. Fleming always wrote rapidly, in part because he was not meticulous about revision; *Casino Royale* was realized in so short a time because he did no research for it. It came straight from "memory and imagination" (Pearson, p. 191). He shrugged it off to friends and others as a joke between himself and the reading public—thus, he maintained the pose of the talented, cavalier Etonian gentleman who could dash off best-sellers with casual ease. According to the author, James Bond was not really a character in *Casino Royale*—more a clothes dummy, a mouth-piece, a zombie. The book had, in the author's later opinion, a lot of description, but the main characters were "dreadfully banal" (Pearson, p. 206). Self-denigration, of course, is one of the characteristics of the detached personality.

Even after he had become something of a celebrity—his books were beginning to sell well, and the movie producers Broccoli and Saltzman were interested in filming his novels—Fleming felt insecure in his new role as a public figure. Why did these feelings develop in Fleming? There was first of all his family situation—an illustrious older sibling, a famous and much-admired father, a strong-willed mother who kept the glorious legend of the father alive. He could never shake loose from the dominance, real and imagined, that his family exerted over him. His restlessness at schools, Tennerhof as well as Eton and Sandhurst, show the young man in rebellion against his mother's influence and control. His reactions took the form of rejecting the "right schools," and also the "right" attitudes toward women, especially after the in-terrupted engagement. The pose that nothing in life matters, that all accomplishments are effortlessly attained, allowed the young Fleming to distance himself from life. By refusing to become involved with people, he could protect himself from further intrusions. He could become the master of his own fate, impervious to frustrations and pain.

Fleming's destiny denied him the life of a man of action that he would like to have lived. During the war as a desk-bound administra-tor for the Office of the Naval Intelligence, for instance, he seldom had the opportunity to act athletically. Yet he apparently told people that he had been in wartime France before its fall and that he had assisted in the evacuation of civilians, French as well as English, before the German armies arrived.

If this account is true, he did have some opportunity for action; we are skeptical of this story, however, and do not want to draw any conclusion about Fleming's life from it. If he chose never to enter active combat, he is not to be censured for this. He was, after all, an officer of Naval Intelligence, and he had no business risking his neck in combat, or worse, getting captured by the enemy and being forced to reveal under torture any part of the information that was stored in his brain.

The life of his idealized spy James Bond may have been incredibly vigorous and physical, but for Fleming himself the reality consisted of some skiing, a bit of mountain climbing (mainly in his adolescence and young manhood), and golf—mainly the latter—which were the extent of his physical activities in his later years. From his adolescence there had been a physical, athletic, side to him. As a young man he loved to ski and to mountain-climb. He was an avid golfer—as any reader of *Goldfinger* could tell. In Jamaica he loved to snorkel, and when he was there would go in for an exploratory swim nearly every day. From this experience scenes from *Dr. No, Thunderball,* and *Live and Let Die* emerged. But James Bond is portrayed as an expert skier, scuba diver, and hang glider, jet and helicopter pilot, high speed racing driver, sky diver, motorcyclist, and all-around acrobat; in Fleming's mature years, golf was the extent of his physical activity.

Bond is Fleming's wish-fulfillment. In writing about James Bond, Fleming could live out in fantasy the life of courage and involvement that he denied himself in reality. Bond enabled Fleming to realize the detached personality's paradoxical dream of achievement without really trying. He could sneer at Bond while his secret agent was making him famous. He wanted to be accepted by intellectuals, the kind of people Ann knew so well, whom he feared sneered at him. He socialized with the likes of W. Somerset Maugham (who had been a secret agent for Her Majesty's government in Russia at the time of the Revolution), Evelyn Waugh, Malcolm Muggeridge, Cyril Connolly, Peter Quennell, Sir Isiah Berlin, and Duff Cooper. He had imposed upon many of his influential friends and acquaintances to promote the sales of *Casino Royale,* but later he wanted their approval of the book—and of his subsequent books. In January 1955 Noel Coward confided to his diary that he wished that Ian would "try a non-thriller for a change. I would so love him to triumph over the sneers of Annie's intellectual friends" (Benson, p. 55). Fleming affected to despise intellectuals, but at heart he wanted their acclaim. He was especially delighted when Raymond

Chandler, the American hard-boiled detective fiction writer, praised his writing in 1955. It revived Fleming's flagging faith in his own work and self-worth.

Throughout his life, the creator of James Bond was very much a creature of upper-class values. Ernest Cuneo's assessment is so incisive that it is worth repeating here: he understood that Fleming was easily understood, "but only within the complex class structure of the British civilization into the upper stratum of which he was born" (Benson, p. xi). But Fleming had little insight into his own character or his own limitations. For example, he once wrote to a friend that he was a popular writer because his public liked to read about cars and gold (Pearson, p. 312). Yet he was baffled and resentful when early critics chastised him about his snobbishness. When they also complained about his preoccupation with sex and sadism, he had to plead guilty to those charges. Yet today his presentations of sexuality and violence would seem quite mild.

Fleming strove for orderliness in the details of his life—in his job, his politics (he was an avid Tory), his personal relations with friends (and tolerated acquaintances), and his writing habits. When writing, he kept to a rigid schedule, typing so many pages a day and quitting work at the same time every day. He attempted to make order in the world around him, and dreaded chaos. Order was the basic, essential state from which he felt that he could occasionally depart, as with his occasional forays into innovative behavior while on one or another of his journalistic assignments abroad. Riots that he witnessed in Istanbul appalled him; they thrust a chaotic world under his chin for the first time in his life, and, what was the more galling, he could not do anything about it.

Chapter Three
Fleming's Life as a Spy

The recruitment of Ian Fleming for the position of personal assistant to the director of Naval Intelligence is in several ways an encapsulation of his own life in British society and an emblem of a certain stratum of British life. Fleming's wartime boss, Rear Adm. John H. Godfrey, was taken from sea duty in August 1939 to head the Division of Naval Intelligence (DNI). He was at that time only fifty years old and due to end his tour of duty on the battle-cruiser *Repulse,* and he had never given serious thought to a career in naval intelligence. He was an admiral who always put to sea, who had never polished doorknobs in the Queen's navy.

The Division had been allowed to deteriorate after World War I, and with a new conflict seemingly imminent, it had been decided that the British Intelligence establishment would be rebuilt. When Sir Reginald ("Blinker") Hall had been its commanding officer, ONI had enjoyed the reputation of being the premier Intelligence service in the world. The job had its traditional glamour, and the director enjoyed a status that exceeded that of his opposite numbers, the director of Military Intelligence and the chief of air staff (Intelligence)—for the admiralty controlled the navy at sea.

Rear Admiral Godfrey had substantial experience in naval operations when he left the fleet. He had served on the China Station patrolling the Yangtze River. In the Dardanelles strait campaign he had served as a navigator and staff officer. He had been chief-of-staff to Commodore Burmeister of the Mediterranean Command. In this last capacity he had overseen the running of local Intelligence centers and been involved in the first experiments with the convoy system. As commander of the *Repulse* he was evaluated by his commander-in-chief as "one captain who knows how to behave like an admiral." And so when the official offer came to him, Godfrey did not express another preference (MacLachlan, pp. 12–14).

One of his first tasks was to assemble a staff. As Pearson so aptly puts it, "the usual mode of entry to the misty world of intelligence is by knowing somebody who knows somebody, and there was an impressive cluster of people . . . who knew Ian Fleming well" (p. 92). Adm. Aubrey Hugh-Smith, who had been deputy director under Blinker Hall in World War I, had known Fleming at the stockbrokerage firm of Rowe and Pitman. Godfrey had also consulted the brokerage firm of Baring Brothers, whose chairman had close ties with Robert Fleming's firm. Senior partner Hugo Pitman was one of Fleming's friends; yet it must be assumed that he recommended Fleming on personal grounds since he thought him "among the world's worst" stockbrokers (Pearson, p. 74). The old ties held; a predecessor of Fleming's was Sir Claude Serocold, who had been personal assistant to director Sir Reginald Hall and who had known the Flemings for many years. Earlier, Hall had chosen a stockbroker for his assistant; Godfrey, emulating what must have seemed to him a successful tradition, did the same.

Such procedures have not been without their critics. John Le Carré, who spent some time in the Foreign Office, has written about the recruits of Britain's SIS (explaining the background of the Kim Philby phenomenon) and their political monasticism (in Knightley, pp. 86–87):

Within its own walls, its clubs, and its country houses, in whispered luncheons with its secular contacts, it would enshrine the mystical entity of a vanishing England. Here, at least, whatever went on in the big world outside, England's flower would be cherished. "The Empire may be crumbling; but within our secret elite, the clean-limbed tradition of English power would survive. We believe in nothing but ourselves."

Still, before making an irrevocable decision, Godfrey wanted to see the man "live." Fleming was accordingly invited to lunch with the admiral at the popular Carlton Grill. The encounter went splendidly. As Pearson describes it (pp. 92–93), "the charm, the vitality, the sense of adventure and enthusiasm" of this thirty-year-old won the older man over. Ian's confidence, his "air of authority," were impressive; they would be needed in the admiralty, where he would have to work with and direct naval officers many years his senior. At lunch Rear Admiral Godfrey suggested that Fleming hold himself in readiness for a "special post" should the next war come. The director was satisfied that he had identified his man.

Many of the operatives in British intelligence were recruited from the ranks of the wealthy middle- and upper classes. They were considered inherently loyal to Britain, it being inconceivable that those who owed so much to the present British societal structure would ever betray that society. In Phillip Knightley's history of twentieth-century espionage, *The Second Oldest Profession*, one former member of SIS recalled that

the whole organization was riddled with nepotism . . . dim, dreary people of utter unmemorability; sub-men who were doubled up with other sub-men to create an illusion of strength and only doubled the weakness; others [made] memorable only by poisonous, corrupt, malevolence or crass, mulish stupidity; the whole run by a chain of command remarkable for its feebleness. The entire service was decrepit and incompetent. (p. 115)

The historian Hugh Trevor-Roper, who joined SIS during the war, was equally appalled by the quality of the prewar recruits:

It seemed to me that the professionals were by and large pretty stupid and some of them very stupid. They formed two social classes: the London end which consisted of elegant young men from the upper classes who were recruited on the basis of trust, within a social class. It is said that they were recruited in Boodles and Whites. I believe this to be basically true. . . . Then there were the Indian policemen. . . . They were rather looked down on. (in Knightley, p. 87)

Several days after the Carlton Grill interview Ian Fleming received official notification from the secretary of the admiralty: ". . . My lords have given directions that you should be earmarked for service under the Admiralty in the event of emergency" (Pearson, pp. 92–93). Although ostensibly still a full-time stockbroker, the young recruit began his on-the-job training several afternoons a week. After mornings at Rowe and Pitman, he would walk along the Mall to the Admiralty Quadrangle, and once inside make his way to Room 39, one of the most famous addresses in Intelligence history. The first sea lord's office was above; the private entrance to No. 10 Downing Street was just on the other side of the square. It was soon to become the nerve center of wartime naval operations and Ian Fleming was to play a vital role in its functioning.

Another important spy agency established in England during wartime, in June 1940, was the Special Operations Executive (SOE). This organization was charged with carrying on overt as well as covert operations against Nazi Germany. Its top ranks were immediately filled with Oxbridge men and women, recruited in the established traditions of various secret services from London's elite. Its first head was a former India merchant, his successor a banker. By and large it was officered by stockbrokers, successful businessmen, insurance underwriters, and merchant bankers. By birth and the inclination of their business experience, they were all politically conservative (Knightley, p. 121). Churchill's poetically phrased mission for SOE was to "set Europe ablaze." But a revolution on the Continent might eventually bring the Communists to power, since they were the only alternative political structure in Europe aside from the Fascists and the Nazis. The English establishment, of course, found that alternative unacceptable; hence its incestuous self-perpetuating and self-aggrandizing recruitment of socially prominent, conservative men and women for key wartime intelligence posts.

So, by an aristocratic infrastructural procedure that was to serve him well throughout his life, Fleming's connections made possible an important and socially prominent career. In this instance, it should be noted, he did not seek the position of personal assistant to the director, nor is there any reason to believe that he was even aware of its availability. But when the opening became active, he was there—as a friend of a friend of somebody. This was the way British society worked, and it was the way that many of England's leaders were chosen.

Fleming adjusted well to his new assignments. Donald MacLachlan, who worked with Fleming in Room 39, has written that Fleming's great gift was for "running things" and for drafting memos. He also found Fleming to be a "skilled fixer and a vigorous showman" (1968, p. 8). Fleming did run things well. And his skill at drafting memos, rapidly, with precision and clarity is no insignificant talent, especially in an administrator. As a "skilled fixer" he employed the tact and great charm of which he was capable. These qualities he often discarded in later years, but during the war, when his country needed them, he used them.

He had many ideas about how to win the war. Good or bad, at least they were all imaginative. One skeptic, Admiral Denning, remembered that "a lot of Ian's ideas were just plain crazy," and colleagues soon became accustomed to an element of wildness in Fleming's schemes. Pearson cites Denning's remark (p. 101) that a lot of Fleming's farfetched ideas had just enough glimmer of feasibility to make one think twice before tossing them into a wastebasket. He had in mind Fleming's notion on the eve of the Dieppe raid, for instance, to sink a hollow block of concrete in the Channel, with periscopes for the enclosed crew whose mission it would be to signal about German ship movements. Los Angeles *Times* film critic Leonard Klady, in a multi-page article on Fleming on the occasion of the opening of *The Living Daylights,* reports that one of his wartime ideas had the admiralty freezing clouds, anchoring them to England's coast, and mounting anti-aircraft gun platforms on them. Klady remarks drily that the idea was rejected because it was thought to be "unworkable" (26 July 1987, "Calendar," p. 3). MacLachlan remembers that in Fleming's department there was even "a brief flirtation with astrology" (p. 7).

His accomplishments as assistant to director Rear Admiral Godfrey were such that Godfrey became a great admirer of Fleming's abilities. Even before the beginning of the war—which many felt certain was coming—the director's assistant was at his side in meetings on the highest level. When he stepped down as director of Naval Intelligence in December 1942, Godfrey's evaluation of his assistant was that Fleming had conducted himself "very greatly to my satisfaction. His zeal, ability, and judgment are altogether exceptional, and have contributed very largely to the development, and organization of the Naval Intelligence Division during the war. Any further remarks would be superfluous" (Pearson, p. 127). Elsewhere, Godfrey is quoted by MacLachlan as calling Fleming "a war-winner" (1968, p. 10).

A few years into the war Rear Admiral Godfrey was relieved of his office, scapegoated (so Knightley believes, p. 170) for the failure of the Merchant Marine to secure its communications adequately, thus giving German submarines throughout much of the war an accurate reading on the movements of Allied convoys. Knightley believes that part of the blame should be given to the Government Code and Cypher School at Bletchley, the agency ostensibly responsible for cipher security. In any event, Godfrey was the only officer of his rank and length of service not to be officially recognized at the war's end.

After Godfrey was replaced—he became flag officer, Royal Indian Navy—Fleming's prestige waned rapidly. Godfrey's managerial style had been to give his subordinates as much latitude as the situation would allow; under this policy, Fleming was constantly at his commander's right hand. The replacement, Commodore E. G. N. Rushbrooke, had a different managerial style, one that made subordinates more closely and directly responsible to their superiors. Fleming became what in fact his title had always indicated—a personal assistant to the director.

Commander Fleming operated from a desk in Room 39 placed in front of the entrance to the director's door. Sefton Delmer remembered the outer workshop (whose admiralty title was N.I.D. 17) as being like a "vast barn," which he later said reminded him of "Arab banks I had visited in Tangier and Beirut." Fleming was the chief clerk in this "bank," sitting near the boss's door, while the other "clerks" "beavered away at stacks of papers" (1962, p. 71). The vast barn was known among the staff as "the zoo" (p. 2). "We were all of us pen-pushers," MacLachlan later recounted (Pearson has the remark coming from Fleming's colleague, Edward Merritt, who is reputed to have prefaced it with the intensifier that Fleming was not James Bond [p. 108]).

At off-duty parties, such affairs as those at which the new lieutenant commander might meet Ann Rothermere, Delmer remembered a very spiffy Ian Fleming "now very important . . . as Personal Assistant of the Director of Naval Intelligence at the Admiralty" (1962, p. 23). And socially, MacLachlan's recollections were of a "giant among name-droppers" (p. 9). MacLachlan thought Fleming's real achievement "was to set a standard of independent, critical and forceful behaviour by RNVR officers" who were suddenly thrust into very important roles to play in the war (p. 10).

The director and his assistant personally initiated a number of clan-destine operations: cutting off the flow of Swedish iron and steel into Nazi Germany, blocking up the Danube, interrupting the stream of Romanian oil into the Reich, briefing double agents (McLachlan, pp. 6–7). Fleming drafted nearly all of the director's important memos. Churchill used to address correspondence to his subordinates—that is, nearly everyone—with the locution, "Pray tell me . . . ," or "Pray, why did 'so-and-so' occur." Replies to Churchill were drafted by Fleming and nearly always forwarded as written to the prime minister. His talent drafting memos was, as already noted, no mean skill. Later, in the United States, Fleming would be credited with drafting an outline of the then hypothetical structure of the forthcoming American OSS, and to have written the entire document in a very short time.

Fleming was an admirer of heroic action—but less the action itself than the idea of it. He voluntarily participated in an espionage training program class on assassinations, but failed at the crucial moment of pulling the trigger because he "couldn't kill a man that way." Ironically, as Pearson remarks (pp. 195–96), he liked to imagine that he had killed someone in the line of duty. William Stephenson thought that he did not have "the temperament for an agent or a genuine man of action" (Pearson, p. 121). The first real violence that Fleming witnessed close at hand was the Istanbul riots, which he witnessed in September 1955. This evocation of the "threat of doom" is said to have "nauseated" him, standing as a horrifying experience for an obsessively ordered mind that reeled before the "apprehension of chaos" (Pearson, p. 271).

During the war, as a desk-bound administrator for Naval Intelligence, Fleming seldom had the opportunity to act courageously. He once wrote that he managed to convince Rear Admiral Godfrey to send him to the west coast of France (primarily to meet with Admiral Darlan about the future of the French fleet); while there, Fleming later claimed, he assisted in the evacuation of French civilians as well as English people caught on the Continent in the panic to escape the rapidly advancing Germans. He credited himself with much of the administration of the evacuation, even to the detail of seeing that the late-arriving King Zog of Albania (with his family and assorted luggage including the Albanian crown jewels) was safely gotten off French land and onto an evacuation vessel (Pearson, p. 105). This, after all of the ships had been loaded with refugees and had already steamed off.

"I cannot imagine what made me suggest this," Fleming is supposed to have said, "except perhaps my usual desire to escape from Room 39 and get some fresh air" (Pearson, p. 102). Pearson does not say where this comment of Fleming's appears, but it is curious. Other biographers do not mention anything about the liaison mission on the Continent, and usually the point is made that Fleming spent the entire war behind his desk. That Godfrey would let one of his most trusted assistants venture into a war zone, with the chance of capture, torture, and the revelation of a treasure of British Intelligence secrets seems unlikely. In the absence of corroborating testimony, this adventure may be put down to Fleming's well-known imagination and wishful fantasizing.

Fleming in the fashion of Thurber's Walter Mitty, fantasized a heroic life through his invented character, James Bond. He himself saw in his hero not only his own projections but those of all "who watch but do not do" (Pearson, p. 200). As the personal assistant to the director of Naval Intelligence, he was primarily a desk warrior. Fleming "wasn't

James Bond," Edward Merritt commented deflatingly, he was just another pen-pusher. All during the war he avoided action and genuine discomfort, fighting the Germans instead with great acts of the imagination.

One of Fleming's most productive ideas came to him after his study of the German occupation of Crete. There, German airborne Intelligence commandoes under the command of Otto Skorzeny (possibly the original model of Hugo Drax) had made directly for a cache of Allied secret documents while the shooting was still going on. Fleming's idea materialized in the creation of No. 30 Assault Unit, whose greatest triumph during the war was the capture of the whole archives of the German Naval Staff (McLachlan, p. 3). Fleming is usually credited with the idea of organizing this crack intelligence commando unit. Based on what he had heard about the Skorzeny assault unit, he suggested that under the command of N.I.D. a similar unit should be organized. He was certainly in a position to see the unit through to operational status. When it was formed and activated, No. 30 Assault Unit—familiarly called by Fleming "My Red Indians"—was to be an effective Intelligence-gathering apparatus.

Skorzeny and his men parachuted into Crete with the first assault troops (the island was captured entirely by airborne troops, a military historical first). They may have been combat-qualified, but their mission on Crete was to seize British headquarters as quickly as possible and to capture as much Intelligence material as possible before the British could destroy it. When they entered British headquarters, they knew exactly what to look for: codes, maps, secret hardware, operational orders, orders of battle, etc. Their skill, their speed, and their preparedness gave them a great success. Later in the war Skorzeny and his men carried out the even more audacious mission of rescuing Mussolini from his captors. They were more than Intelligence commandoes; specially and highly trained, airborne and (what we would now call) Ranger-qualified, this German special unit carried out a number of missions of great importance. What impressed Fleming most was that they did their work with panache.

When the great raid at St. Nazaire was in the planning stage, Fleming had wanted to insert an "assault unit" (he thought of them as "Intelligence scavengers") among the first wave of troops. The idea was rejected. Such a highly trained unit was not yet available. But later, at Dieppe, Fleming's ideas were given a chance. Still, the notion of an assault unit had not been given enough time. Fleming chose two navy lieutenants, gave them command of ten Royal Marines, and outlined a plan for them to fight their way into German headquarters where they would (it was hoped) find and capture German Intelligence materials. Fleming asked to go with them (Pearson, p. 124), but Godfrey refused; he would not risk losing an officer who knew so much classified material. The Dieppe mission failed. The assaulting troops sustained very heavy casualties from the first, never succeeded in getting any kind of toehold on the French coasts, and No. 30 Assault Unit never reached shore.

Still, the idea was deemed a good one. Fleming arranged to get his "Red Indians" specially trained in such skills as forcing safes, picking locks, and the most effective use of explosives, and he procured them crash courses in booby traps, land mines, plastique, and the like. He showed them the kind of thing he wanted them to look for when they went ashore: cyphers, confidential orders, the plans for new weapons, technical information on such things as radar. Since the next Allied invasion was to be in North Africa, Fleming boned up on Algiers, particularly where enemy headquarters was thought to be.

30 Assault Unit was put ashore at the wrong place, in an area not at all like what their briefings had led them to anticipate. But they improvised. Stealing a truck, they rode around until they came across a building that looked like their models of Italian naval headquarters. The Italians were completely surprised, not only by the Allied invasion but especially by the sudden appearance of No. 30 Assault Unit. Enemy documents of various kinds fell into Allied hands and were forwarded to London. Fleming's wild scheme had paid off, in a manner at least as swashbuckling and improbable as his novels. 30 Assault Unit had been the first into enemy territory, successfully invaded the enemy's headquarters, and had captured piles of classified documents before the dazed defenders could destroy them.

Commodore Rushbrooke, Admiral Godfrey's replacement, had less patience with Fleming's adventurous schemes. Control of No. 30 Assault Unit was gradually handed over to others, though its growth (to about 150 men at the time of the Normandy invasions) is an accurate index of the esteem in which it was held by the higher echelons of the admiralty. But it was Fleming who gave them their final D-Day instructions (Pearson, p. 129). They were to land at the Arromanches beachhead and capture the German radar stationed there. They succeeded; but for several months after they were unable to seize any documents of value. One of the reasons seems to be the promptness with

which the Germans destroyed or spirited away classified documents
when they were in danger of falling into enemy hands. Another seems
to be that the men of No. 30 Assault Unit were much like the heroes
of Fleming's imagination: adventurous, independent, preferring real
fighting to the work they were supposed to be doing. They began to
slip out of the control of headquarters in London. Fleming was so in-
furiated by their action that he wired the unit's field commander,
saying:

> I urge you not to continue questioning the decisions of D.N.I. . . . under
> whose orders you operate. The position in Brittany and also in regard to Paris
> is perfectly clear here and we are fully informed on the progress of the cam-
> paign. Why you should imagine that this is not so, which is the only possible
> excuse for your attitude, I cannot understand. The duties of the Unit and its
> immediate role are also planned on the basis of more information than you
> can ever possess in the field. (Pearson)

Shortly after the D-Day invasions, Fleming did manage to inspect No.
30 Assault Unit in the field, and make some attempt to bring it back
under his control, but he never completely succeeded.

30 Assault Unit had one last success in the war, and it was almost
entirely Fleming's doing. As the war was winding down, Fleming
heard that at the castle of Tambach, in the Wuerttemburg forest, lived
an "elderly German Admiral" who owned a tremendous collection of
books and other materials about which Fleming was enormously curious. With fellow officer Trevor Glanville, he drove to Tambach, and
there found the old fellow, who was expecting the Russians momen-
tarily, about to set fire to his entire hoard. The papers were, it turned
out, the complete German Naval archives since 1870. Fleming arrived,
so the story goes (Pearson, p. 133), got on well with the old boy, and
charmed him into saving the documents. Fleming was able to get the
archives in their entirety out of Tambach, first to Hamburg, and then
on to London.

It was in France, while sharing rations with friend Robert Harling,
that Fleming stated what he intended to do after the war: he would
"write the spy story to end all spy stories" (Pearson, p. 131). Harling
said that he "almost choked on [his] Spam." But wherever Fleming
was, in those days, his imagination brought life. In June 1941, on a
secret mission to the United States, Admiral Godfrey and Fleming

stopped over in Lisbon. Godfrey took advantage of their time in Lisbon
to contact his agents there. At night, the two men took advantage of
the capitol's nightlife. On the second night they went to a casino where
Fleming, a cautious gambler, began to steadily lose all that he had
with him. It is reported to have been a dull evening (Pearson, p.
113), with only a small handful of bored locals present, playing for low stakes
before equally bored croupiers. Fleming began to play, and Godfrey
noted "a sort of glazed look" clouding his eyes. Then, suddenly, Fleming whispered, "just suppose those fellows were German agents—what
a coup it would be if we cleaned them out entirely." Break the Nazi
Lisbon Intelligence station, presumably. Godfrey was not engaged.
Nevertheless, Fleming continued at the game for much of the evening
until he was himself wiped out. The Portuguese businessmen (or idlers)
were not Nazi agents in Godfrey's mind, or in anybody else's except
Fleming's, but he remained consistent with his own imagination.

It is thought that this incident provided the idea for the tension-
ridden struggle in *Casino Royale* in which Bond pits himself against Le
Chiffre. That titanic battle (with more than faint overtones of Alex-
ander Pope's mock epic, *The Rape of the Lock*) is the dramatic center of
this first novel. In the fiction, the room is noisy and smoky from the
many excited and voluble players. Tension is running as high as the
stakes, and the calculating yet risk-taking James Bond sits across
the table from a masterful opponent with great resources. Furthermore,
the situation is deliciously complicated by the involvement in the game
of the luscious Vesper Lynd, with whom Bond is instantly smitten.
Further still, when Bond is cleaned out, C.I.A. agent/friend Felix
Leiter comes to his rescue with a fresh bundle. But when Fleming lost
his pocket money in Lisbon, the night simply ended. Not with a bang
but a whimper.

The trip to the United States was an important one for the future
novelist. Ideas were careening around his brain wildly as he assimilated
his new experiences and absorbed his encounters with the famous and
powerful. One of the powerful—rich but not famous, by design—was
Sir William Stephenson, the man variously called "the quiet Canadian"
or popularly "Intrepid" (Nigel West informs us that this was not his
codename, but that of the mission)—one of whose recollections of
Fleming was that he was "always fascinated by gadgets." On that visit
to Washington, in 1941, accompanying Godfrey on a mission of considerable importance, which included giving technical advice on the
establishment of an American secret service (to become the OSS),
Fleming witnessed a raid on the Japanese consulate in Radio City, and

the compromise of the codebooks cached there. Sir William enabled Fleming to be an observer of the complete operation.

It was known that the Japanese counsel-general in New York, located in the RCA Building, was transmitting messages back to Tokyo. In order to facilitate the decoding of these messages, Stephenson clandestinely raided the Japanese office. The cypher clerk's habits were studied carefully. Duplicate keys to the consul-general's office were prepared, and at 3 A.M. of THE day, the break-in was made. The safe was easily cracked, and the codebooks borrowed for about an hour while they were microfilmed back in a British lab, and then returned, with everything replaced in its previous position and condition. Fleming witnessed the entire process. He appears to have been thrilled by the excitement of a real cloak-and-dagger operation. It made enough of an impression on him for its use in *Casino Royale*; when Vesper Lynd praises him for the honor of being one of the few to be entrusted with the "OO" in his identity code, Bond makes a modest disclaimer: "It's not difficult to get a Double O number if you're prepared to kill people," he says. "That's all the meaning it has. It's nothing to be particularly proud of. I've got the corpses of a Japanese cipher expert in New York and a Norwegian double agent in Stockholm to thank for being a Double O. Probably quite decent people" (pp. 58–59). Later, he tells the whole story to his counterpart in French Intelligence, Mathis:

Well, in the last few years I've killed two villains. The first was in New York—a Japanese cipher expert cracking our codes on the thirty-sixth floor of the R.C.A. Building in Rockefeller Center, where the Japs had their consulate. I took a room on the fortieth floor of the next-door skyscraper, and I could look across the street into his room and see him working. Then I got a colleague from our organization in New York and a couple of Remington thirty-thirty's with telescopic sights and silencers. We smuggled them up to my room and sat for days waiting for our chance. He shot at the man a second before me. His job was only to blast a hole through the window so that I could shoot the Jap through it. . . . As I expected, his bullet got deflected by the glass and went God knows where. But I shot immediately after him, through the hole that he had made. I got the Jap in the mouth as he turned to gape at the broken window. (p. 133)

Not all the improbable ideas in the war were Fleming's, of course. When it became known to Stephenson's unit that the French were planning on caching all of their national gold on the island of Martinique for the war's duration, Stephenson (or one of his aides) suggested that the British raid the island and take possession of the bullion in order to finance their European operations. The gold, according to the followup portion of this suggestion, was to be kept on Martinique, but under British control. The idea for *Goldfinger* is said to have begun here (Stevenson, p. 354).

While still in North America, Fleming was invited by his future friend William Stephenson to visit his secret training camp for covert operations. It was near Toronto, on the shore of Lake Ontario. Here the eventual creator of James Bond learned much about the tactics and techniques for espionage and clandestine warfare. The village (Oshawa) was run by several experienced underwater and hand-to-hand combat experts; Allied (as well as American) agents were being trained there, and Sir William thought that Fleming would profit from the experience. He had no idea of one of the ways in which he would literally profit, however.

Experts taught their students the intricacies of cyphers and of code-breaking, silent breaking and entering, the use of radio transmission and detection, and the nitty-gritty of espionage work: how to track down a man and kill him. The friend of the boss was given a condensed tour of the base and its programs. Fleming even joined in some of the fun himself. Not surprisingly, he did best at the underwater exercises, as Bond would later do in *Live and Let Die* and *Doctor No*. Fleming also tried his hand at various small arms and is said to have excelled at the submachine gun. He learned judo. He excelled in one exercise in which he was to plant a "bomb" in a Toronto power station: Fleming called the director, introduced himself as a visiting British engineer, and easily penetrated the station grounds. As a game of covert war, it was a triumph, though it had little carryover to the real war.

Asked about Fleming as a secret agent some years later, Stephenson thought that while he was an exceptional trainee, "he just hadn't got the temperament for an agent or a genuine man of action" (Pearson, p. 121). It was not that Fleming lacked courage; it was just that he had too much imagination. Fleming's last assignment at Oshawa was to track down his target who was put in a cheap Toronto hotel. Stephenson had set up the game as a "test of nerve when it came down to it" (Pearson, p. 121). For the exercise, trainee Fleming was given a pistol loaded with live ammunition. He tracked his "victim" (an expert trained to "dodge" bullets) to the right hotel, entered, and waited outside his room, reviewing his orders to shoot to kill. After an unusually long wait, Fleming emerged without having fired a shot. As he explained to Stephenson, "I just couldn't open that door. I couldn't kill a man that way" (Pearson, p. 121).

While in his Naval Intelligence office he often met Churchill, for some periods on a daily basis; in the United States he also met J. Edgar Hoover, whom he described as "a chunky man with slow eyes and a trap of a mouth" who "firmly but politely [said he was] uninterested in our mission" (Pearson, p. 114). Hoover was anything but uninterested in the visit of the British Intelligence agents. America was in the process of considering its own Intelligence agency (to succeed its peacetime coordinating Officer of Intelligence), and the chief of the FBI was jockeying for power in its formation and operation. He did not want to complicate, and presumably vitiate, his strength with separate ties to Naval Intelligence. But Fleming seems not to have been aware of the internal struggles in the United States. Bureaucratic skirmishes never held much interest for him.

Though never involved in real, life-threatening action he admired those who were, and envied them their activity. Though he could involve himself wholeheartedly in war games, he did not have the stomach to kill. As a game, war could be exciting because while it was not really dangerous, it was mentally as well as physically challenging; but when it became more than a game, or more than a fiction, war was sinister, shocking, revolting, disabling. Not a daring gambler himself, Fleming saw the attractiveness of daring, and gave that daring to James Bond. He endowed Bond with many of the qualities he had admired in his own life as a boy, many of those he encountered in the Naval Intelligence but which, for one reason or another, he never manifested himself. The exciting life, the wild life, the socially amoral life, the undisciplined life—these he allowed James Bond to live for him.

Chapter Four
Ian Fleming, Writer

Though he has been widely read and frequently discussed, Ian Fleming's writing has evoked little critical consensus. Was he a skillful writer or a careless one? An important artist or a popular hack? One reason for this indecisiveness is that so many questions are asked about aspects of his writing other than his craftsmanship; is he (and his character James Bond) a snob? a sadist? a product of the modern consumer-oriented world? Is he a gentleman? a fascist? a sexist? a racist?

A few, including Kingsley Amis and Umberto Eco, have praised his writing talents but most of Fleming's critics have addressed themselves to what has been called the Fleming "phenomenon." Given the prevalent genre snobbism—a contempt for the spy novel and for detective fiction as genres—so much commentary on Fleming and on Bond is unusual. In the 1980s only John Le Carré attracts as much attention—no doubt because, though he is a "spy novelist," he has indisputable talent. But Fleming? His talent *is* disputed and often denigrated. The one facet of his writing that commands attention from critics is his enormous popularity.

Fleming's style has not invited penetrating assessments of James Bond's character and moral philosophy. Something has been made of the influence of clubland heroes Richard Hannay and Bulldog Drummond (from the novels of John Buchan and "Sapper," respectively) on Fleming's writing. But not enough; more will be made of it in this chapter, below. And other aspects of his writing skills will also be examined, his handling of plots, his ability at characterization, his style (particularly diction, narrative balance, humor, etc.), his settings, his place as a writer of an almost entirely exterior world.

Umberto Eco believes that Fleming owes much to Mickey Spillane. At the end of *Casino Royale,* Bond reports to London headquarters on the demise of double agent Vesper Lynd, still thought by London to be loyal (we use the English language version, not Eco's retranslation *On Her Majesty's Secret Service* from the Italian):

"This is 007 speaking. This is an open line. It's an emergency. Can you hear me? . . . Pass this on at once: 3030 was a double, working for Redland. . . .

"Yes, dammit, I said was. The bitch is dead now." (*CR*, p. 180)

Eco states confidently that in a Spillane novel Mike Hammer would have killed her himself. In *Casino,* Vesper takes her own life. But Bond's reaction is what Hammer's would have been: love immediately turns to hate, tenderness to violence (Eco, p. 35).

Just as Hemingway's World War I battlefield traumatic wound was to influence nearly all of his writing, so—in Eco's reading—*Casino Royale* set a structural pattern for the rest of Fleming's writing. Eco actually cites Hammer's haunting memories of a Japanese he had killed during the war, which influences all of his subsequent adventures. The reasoning is weak here: one wounding actually happened to the author, the other to his character only. We do not know if Spillane had ever been in combat, nor if he was haunted by images of murder. We do know that Fleming had been in Rockefeller Center when William Stephenson's men entered the Japanese consulate to copy the codebook there; in *Casino Royale* Fleming transforms that reality into an assassination in which Bond fires the lethal bullet from an adjacent skyscraper. Eco thinks that this episode is seminal. However, Bond does not suffer the neurosis Spillane has Hammer suffer; Fleming excludes it from the narrative, thus "curing" Bond by nontherapeutic means. "This decision was to influence the structure of the following eleven novels by Fleming and presumably forms the basis for their success" (Eco, p. 36).

Fleming declared, after the publication of *Doctor No,* that having found a formula he was comfortable with, he was going to use it for the rest of his novels. The statement was probably made out of anger at the critics' response to his first several novels, but subsequent books did adhere to the structural pattern established in *Doctor No.* Basically, at the beginning of the masterplot Bond is made aware of the villain's stronghold, which is physically isolated from the rest of the world. In *Doctor No* it is his island off Jamaica; Mr. Big has his own Caribbean island as well. Blofeld's fortress (in *You Only Live Twice*) is in Asia. In the earlier *On Her Majesty's Secret Service,* Blofeld maintained a Alpine retreat. Goldfinger has a carefully guarded plot of land in central Europe. *Moonraker's* Hugo Drax's secret installation is on the Dover Coast. As the masterplot unfolds, Bond penetrates the villain's fortress, sometimes with the woman in tow; he is usually captured, but escapes (or endures torture and is released) and captures or kills the villain almost immediately afterward.

Eco's master template for the structure of the Bond novels (p. 52 ff.), although at variance with the writer's declared intention, offers more insight into Fleming's plotting. (It was D. H. Lawrence who said, Trust the tale, not the teller.) In Eco's "monoplot," the action begins when a) "M" assigns a task to Bond; b) the villain is made known to Bond, who c) closes with him/her and one or the other gives a "first check"; d) the woman is in contact with Bond, who e) seduces her at once or else makes a seduction gambit; f) Bond is captured by the villain (sometimes with the woman, though their captures may occur at different times); and g) Bond is tortured by the villain. Bond triumphs, however, in h) killing either him or his agent. While recuperating i) Bond "enjoys" the woman, whom he eventually loses. In this formulaic pattern, the episodes move with the inexorability of the common folktale as revealed by Propp's structural analysis.

We can make Eco's "monoplot" even more compact. Bond receives his orders, thereby setting the plot in motion. He makes contact with the villain. Proximity needs no further catalyst: Bond and the villain engage in a "first check." The first departure from this inevitable sequence is the appearance of the woman, and that is followed by another Fleming given, the attempt to seduce her. In the third sequence of this "monoplot," Bond is captured and then tortured (in some variations, the woman is also tortured), but the hero is able to escape and almost immediately after manages to kill the villain. In an epilogue (though perhaps to many readers it is an essential part of the plot) Bond convalesces, simultaneously enjoying the woman.

So much of the Bond novels consists of surface action that we wonder why Umberto Eco (1966) takes so seriously Bond's sickbed conversation with his French Intelligence counterpart, Mathis, at the end of *Casino Royale*. If this conversation is central to Fleming's message, then we have a very different type of novel from those we commonly assume to have been written. Bond wonders about the morality of what they have been doing; have they been fighting for the right? Have their recently defeated enemies also been serving a noble cause? Is there a clearcut distinction between good and evil in their world? The dialogue sounds like watered-down Graham Greene, but Eco thinks, "at this point Bond is ripe for the crisis . . . and he sets off along the route traversed by the protagonist of Le Carré" (p. 36). Mathis's reply is crucial to Bond's development in all of the succeeding novels. When you get back to London, he tells his English colleague, there will be other evils to conquer; now that he has seen an evil man Bond will know other evil men when he sees them, and he will be inspired to go and destroy them. "Surround yourself with human beings, my dear James. They are easier to fight for than principles. But don't let me down and become human yourself. We would lose such a wonderful machine" (p. 37 in Eco; pp. 137–38 in the novel).

After that moment, Eco thinks, Bond's course has been charted. He abandons the "treacherous life of moral meditation" (p. 37), putting all psychological and moral aspects aside. He becomes, and remains consistently throughout the remaining dozen novels, the "wonderful machine." Bond no longer complicates his life with reflections on the nature of good and evil, truth and justice, life and death—except, as Eco remarks sardonically, in moments of boredom, for instance in the bar of an airport. He no longer feels any twinges of doubt; moral qualms never interfere with his subsequent missions, however lethal. Fleming had made a decision, as indicated by Bond's conversation with Mathis, to renounce psychological motivation in the depiction of his hero's adventures, and to replace it with conventional formulas.

In discussing Fleming's characterization of James Bond, one first of all has to confront the author's evaluation of his hero as "that cardboard booby." Many would agree with him; Pearson wrote of *Casino Royale* that the minor characters are "merest shadows with names attached" (p. 198). Bond himself is not a character in this first novel, but a dummy for Fleming "to hang his clothes on, a zombie to perform the dreams of violence and daring which fascinate his creator." But is that an accurate assessment of one of the century's greatest fictional heroes? Is there something more to the cardboard booby? And is he entirely Fleming's invention?

Others have pointed out that Bond's characterization owes much to several enormously popular adventure stories that Fleming probably read as a boy, specifically at Durnford preparatory school, on the isle of Purbeck. These were the novels of Dornford Yates, John Buchan, and H. C. McNeil ("Sapper"), whose Bulldog Drummond Fleming often acknowledged "as the true spiritual forerunner of James Bond" (Pearson, p. 20). And these books were the favorites of more than public schoolboy visionaries. Richard Usborne reported (pp. 1–2) that during his time in the Secret Service in World War II practically every secret service officer he had met imagined himself to be one of Buchan's heroes, either Richard Hannay or Sandy Arbuthnot. What might Fleming have learned from Yates, Buchan, and Sapper?

To begin with, the great game (in Kipling's phrase) and a greater cause. In those thrillers of the 1920s and 1930s the games of the heroes (they were all amateurs at espionage or at criminology) were played on behalf of a higher cause—queen, country, the right. Hannay, Drummond, and Jonah Mansel were all clubmen and landed gentlemen of leisure. Their morality was that of the English public school prefect's room. They usually took the law into their own hands, but it was a righteous taking, because they acted out of a higher nobility (Usborne, pp. 2–10). Pearson thinks even the attitudes of Bond and Hannay toward women were similar: Buchan's hero idealized women and Bond seduced them, but both attitudes served as a means of keeping women out of the real world of men (p. 83).

From Yates, not an espionage or even much of an adventure writer, Fleming might nevertheless have gotten several reinforcements for his own predilections. Owning and driving expensive automobiles was a hobby of Yates's lead male characters; Jonah Mansel, his only secret agent, was the proud owner of a Rolls Royce, which was specially rigged to conceal pistols, rifles, handcuffs, ropes, a medicine chest, etc., all the things that the well-equipped secret agent required for foreign travel. There were no lasers or jet-assisted acceleration systems, of course, as they, like most of the Bond car gadgets, were still in the future—though Mansel did have a "top-secret locker," exact contents unidentified (Usborne, p. 67).

Like Bond, Jonah Mansel frequented his favorite off-the-beaten-track hotels and inns, having many in his repertoire. Like Bond, he had an independent income, having inherited £200,000—a bit more than James had put by. Yates's favorite heroes were not secret agents, but the comfortable, genteel, eminently likeable Pleydell clan. Yet there is something of Bond here, too: Berry Pleydell was said to be "fussy about his wines and spirits;" and Boy Pleydell was a veritable Romeo to his many Juliets (Usborne, pp. 56–60).

But it is the world created by writer John Buchan for his hero Richard Hannay that comes closest to the ambiance of James Bond. The characters of the earlier writer are two-dimensional, always secondary to the plot of the novel of the moment. Hannay especially is the epitome of the outdoorsman, longing often for the invigorating air of the Veldt (he is South African, and the climate of London makes him "liverish"). Buchan's formula for the good life consists of cold baths, hard work, and healthy exhaustion. They are the essentials for mental and spiritual as well as physical health. And Buchan's heroes, like Fleming, went to Eton.

Hannay was not a full-time professional secret service agent; his relation to the secret world was often coincidental (if not accidental), though in the books after *The Thirty-nine Steps* we learn that his wife, Mary, was an officer in the British Secret Service. Hannay's occasional friend is Ted Leithen, gassed during World War I and made a permanent invalid by tuberculosis. Similarly, Bond's CIA friend, Felix Leiter, is a multiple amputee from the several wounds received during his adventures. Another of Buchan's romantic swashbucklers, Sandy Arbuthnot, has some of the seeds of Bond. He played a pretty good game of bridge (anticipating *Moonraker*?), and, like Bond, was not a deep thinker but rather audacious, resourceful, and far-sighted. Buchan's villains, though ominous enough, do not much resemble Fleming's except that they are all foreigners. The earlier writer's villains were not, in Usborne's words, "really juicy fiends" (p. 83). Only one striking similarity stands out: as Blofeld would later attempt to do to a civilian population, Moxon Ivery (of Buchan's *Mr. Standfast*) plans to spread disease (in his case anthrax) throughout the British army.

Sapper's heroes—Bulldog Drummond's trusty crew—were all amateur athletes. Not an egghead among them. Usborne (p. 146) rightly calls them protofascists, for their inclination to bully beaten opponents. Drummond and his best chum, Maitland, revel in "rough-housing" and the thrill of physical danger. They were the ideal heroes of schoolboy's books. A typical day for them follows this plan: a large breakfast, lunch with martinis at the club, a game of golf in the afternoon, then back to the club for dinner, then an evening of poker or "yarning" (Usborne, p. 147). Not exactly Bond's cup of tea, but then he is not the same sort of schoolboy hero; his violence on behalf of the state is institutionalized. That of Drummond and his friends was for the right as God gave them to see the right.

Drummond's pals were known (significantly, though not to Sapper) as "The Breed." They were English clubmen all. Their author glorified the comradeship, leadership, and bravery of the good old days in the trenches. His bad guys, effete of course, liked champagne and caviare (some things were changed when Bond became the hero of clubland).

The Breed were all decent fellows who stood up for the king (as does Bond); the villains were all foreigners—dagos, Russians, Teutons, Jews. Each one of them sought to destroy the British way of life—first through the establishment of trade unions, then through strikes. They were trash, they were factory workers, they were the unwashed. Thus the Breed was morally justified in passionlessly killing those offensive dirty dagos. Sapper was fond of lashing victims to chairs; villain Henry Lakington savages the hero with his hunting-crop after he has lashed Drummond to a chair. Was this scene in the back of Fleming's mind when he wrote *that* scene in *Casino Royale?*

Drummond lived in a world still dominated by Queen Victoria. None of the decent chaps seduced women; rather, the women they were most likely to meet were the kind they would want to marry (and occasionally did), or the elderly pensioned-off nurses, or the dear old housekeepers, loyal to the core (Usborne, p. 149)—like Bond's May? The Bulldog's nurse, Mrs. Penny (Miss Moneypenny's prototype?) was in this mold, retired, though faithful still.

Though Fleming learned from Yates, Buchan, and Sapper, he did not copy their models slavishly. Bond was to be his own literary creation. The similarities are obvious—of character, of detail, of attitude. Yet the times had changed. One thing The Breed would never forgive was cheating at cards (Usborne, p. 185). Bond would be a little more forgiving in such matters; when he exposes Hugo Drax's card deceptions, he is not morally outraged. He does not feel as if some basic human decency has been violated. He works hard, nevertheless, to reveal the cheat, but not with the ire of the self-righteous. In his golf game with Goldfinger, he is not above cheating the cheat, and it all ends as it would have if both had played the game straight from the start. Neither man has great moral complexity, though Fleming's hero is more sensitive on this point than his predecessor. Neither has great intellect. Drummond, like Bond, was not much of a detective; when he tried to think a problem through, it usually "didn't work very well" (Usborne, p. 154).

As with Buchan and Sapper, Fleming's conception—and thus his depictions—of good and evil are rather clearly demarked. England is good, "white men" are good, the king and queen are good, and thus their hard-working agent James Bond is also good. Ranged against him are the bad ones: criminals and gangsters, but mainly communists in their various outward forms—Russian Intelligence officers and their international criminal minions who head up such organizations as SMERSH. The international-conspiracy aspect of some of the villains is slight; what all of the bad ones have in common is that they threaten England.

Eco reads irony in Fleming's style (p. 60 ff.) on the level of the nature and sequence of episodes. This irony is manifest in the "incredibly exaggerated" aspects of the plots: "in *From Russia* his Soviet men are so monstrous, so improbably evil that it seems impossible to take them seriously. And yet in his brief preface Fleming insists that all the atrocities that he narrates are absolutely true." He has taken the path of the fable, Eco concludes, "and fable must be taken as truthful if it is not to become a satirical fairy-tale." Fleming's narratives have two [intentionally crafted] narrative "levels": the literal and the fabulous. Yet the tone is "authentic, credible, ingenious, plainly aggressive." Such a writer, Eco thinks, is an apolitical cynic, "a deviser of tales for general consumption."

Pearson insisted that there was no humor in Fleming's books (pp. 191–92): "The one quality they lack entirely is humour." Each novel, he thought, is "written in deadly seriousness." But some humor in Fleming, quite apart from his monstrous villains, should not be denied. The names of some of his characters certainly were not meant to be taken seriously. The clutch of mobsters that Goldfinger has gathered for his big job, have joke names: Jack Strap, Jed Midnight, Pussy Galore (or the name of the master of ceremonies, Auric Goldfinger himself). Elsewhere we meet with Jack and Seraffimo Spang, Honeychile Rider, Kissy Suzuki, Tiffany Case, Sluggsy and Horror, and Mary Goodnight. Puns, especially in his selection of chapter headings, abound. A cheap form of humor? Perhaps, but it was also Shakespeare's favorite form.

Bond evaluates his chances against Drax's fifty "robots" (*Moonraker,* p. 106); but no, there are now only forty-nine, one having recently been killed with a severe blow to the head—had "blown his top (apt expression, reflected Bond)." One of Mr. Big's hoods (*Live and Let Die,* p. 122) "had small, close-set eyes as cruel as a painless dentist's." Escaping the Spangs' desert fortress with Tiffany Case on a stolen locomotive, the engine starts to give out, and Bond turns to his engineer accomplice:

"Can you get anything more out of this?"

"Not a scrap," she said grimly, "even if my name were Casey Jones instead of Case."

"We'll be all right," said Bond. "You keep her rolling. Maybe he'll blow his stack or something."

"Oh, sure," she said. "Or maybe the spring'll run down and he's left the wind-up key at home in his pants pocket."

After having made good his escape, Bond meets Leiter at the bar of the Beverly Hills Hotel. James's face is battered and scarred from his recent ordeals but, Fleming assures us, he drew no attention in his brand-new Hollywood clothes, for "he might have been a stunt-man with a heavy work load" (p. 173).

In *Goldfinger,* when a mobster gives Bond his word (James is still in disguise as Goldfinger's henchman), the Englishman reflects "the candour was as false as a second-hand motor salesman's" (p. 206). When he is captured on Blofeld's poisonous island and threatened with death in a boiling sulphurous geyser, Bond quips,

Well, Blofeld, you mad bastard. I'll admit that your effects man down below knows his stuff. Now bring on the twelve she-devils, and if they're all as beautiful as Fraulein Bunt [Blofeld's strikingly ugly assistant], we'll get Noel Coward to put it to music and have it on Broadway by Christmas. How about it?

This is one of the very few times that Bond is given such lines of insolent detachment from his captor, though he is certainly captured often enough. If Fleming had wanted to highlight his nonchalance, his coolness under peril and stress, he might have done more of the same. And if he had had the wit. Now, none of the above lines are very funny, but if they were they might have detracted from the prevailing tone of the episodes. The resultant farce was not exactly what Fleming seems to have had in mind. John Cawelti reads in Fleming at least one or two sentences *per page* which hint at "some form of put-on or self-parody" (*Spy Story,* p. 149). Some of this is conscious, we all agree; and some—perhaps most of it—Cawelti says, is unconscious. How much was unconscious? How much of Fleming's put-on humor was a multiform extension of his self-deprecating "cardboard booby" characterization? Something in him wanted to belittle his efforts, but only part of this desire can be traced to his need to maintain the mask of the Etonian gentleman, whose every achievement is effortless. The far larger part, we believe, arises from his need to deny his accomplishments, so as to lessen his inner conflicts about succeeding.

Because Fleming wrote so quickly, some of the more fundamental aspects of his style suffered. He had some problems with diction, for instance. Some words became his favorites and he could not resist using them—again and again and again. "Hiss," filled almost universal functions for him. Machinery hisses: hydraulic garage lifts and doors open with hisses, Dr. No's elevator door hisses open and shut, the doors of the Piz Gloria open and close with a pneumatic hiss, Mercedes hiss along the *Autobahn,* other cars hiss up hills or back down the road, fine old leather upholstery hisses luxuriously when sat on, the brakes of trucks hiss angrily when they careen through quiet villages, blow-torches hiss when lit, vaporized paraffin hisses out its vital tongue of flame, gas space heaters hiss, electricity hisses in Dr. No's torture tube, water hisses past swimmers and out of shower heads onto bathers.

Bond let the smoke from one of his lit Royal Blends hiss between his teeth; thrown knives hiss past their target's head, Bond's canoe hisses into the water; the sun hisses like an orange ball into the sea; skis hiss smoothly through powdered snow; severed ski lift cables hiss down the slopes; black cormorants hiss; cyanide guns hiss.

People hiss commands; murderers hiss when their victims pain them; Bond exhales breath between his clenched teeth with a quiet hiss; Rosa Klebb hisses something at him in Russian; a Chinese woman hisses out some words at Quarrel (probably in English); Bond hisses out a string of obscenities between clenched teeth (at Dr. No); Billy Ring hisses through his teeth like a Japanese when he talked. Hissing seems to be an inevitable result of ordinary Japanese speech, and so occurs frequently in *You Only Live Twice,* where the natives several times "hiss and bow" their ways around, even at the local whorehouse.

"Sighing" is another Fleming favorite. When lift doors do not hiss, they sigh, and if the apparatus is precision-made it will sigh into motion and sigh to a stop, like expensive cars that sigh under way (like Goldfinger's yellow Rolls), or pneumatic doors that emit a pressurized sigh. A hiss is still a hiss, a sigh is but a sigh. These are not startling words to be sure but neither are they lexical choices that wear well when used many times per book. And it should be of interest that "hiss" and "sigh," which are both words commonly used to describe human responses, are almost invariably used by Fleming to simulate the sounds of machines. When humans do hiss—Klebb, a disgusting and ruthless officer of the KGB, or Bond—it is a sound of anger and hostile aggression. "Sigh" is often a sound made by lovers; in Fleming it is never associated with love or passion, only with machines.

Eco (1966, p. 65 ff.) has been the most articulate critic to comment on the balance in Fleming's narratives. By this he means "the minute and leisurely concentration with which he pursues for page after page descriptions of articles, landscapes and events apparently inessential to the course of the story; and conversely the feverish brevity with which he covers in a few paragraphs the most unexpected and improbable actions." Eco cites the example of *Goldfinger*, Fleming's seventh novel, so that he could hardly be excused for inexperience: two pages are given to Bond's meditation on the murder of a Mexican he has committed on assignment before the narrative begins, fifteen pages devoted to the game of golf (the action and competitive drama of which many critics admire, by the way), twenty-five pages lavished on the car trip across France, "as against the four or five pages which cover the arrival at Fort Knox of a false hospital train" (one of the central episodes of the plot, which is, after all, an attack on Fort Knox).

About one-fourth of *Thunderball* is spent in descriptions of the Shrublands health spa's natural diets and cures, their Turkish baths and massages. The time and space devoted to these incidental details is not justified by the plot of the novel. Eco is most incensed by the five pages given to Domino Vitale's description (much of which is her imaginative extension) of a box of Player's cigarettes, and this *after* she has already told Bond her life story. A justified elaboration of detail is found in Bond's preparations for his bridge game with Hugo Drax; together with the development of the party, Fleming allots it thirty pages. In those pages Fleming gradually marshalls his rhetorical forces for the suspense of the game. Domino's rambling does not establish the sort of personal qualities that one would think Fleming would want: an endlessly aimless daydreamer. As Eco says:

. . . it is "aimless" to introduce diamond-smuggling in South Africa in *Diamonds are Forever*, which opens with the description of a scorpion, as though seen through a magnifying glass, enlarged to the size of some prehistoric monster, as the protagonist in a story of life and death at animal level, interrupted by the sudden appearance of a human being who crushes the scorpion. Then the action of the book begins, as though what has gone before represents only the titles, cleverly presented, of a film which then proceeds in a different manner. (p. 66).

Aimlessness also characterizes the beginning of *From Russia, with Love*, which devotes an entire page to a man lying by the side of a pool.

With Fleming we examine Red Grant (though his name is not given and his role in the plot is not indicated), while a blue and green dragonfly scrutinizes his body "pore by pore, hair by hair" (p. 66).

But actually Eco is an admirer of Fleming's techniques. He insists that such passages are not accidental—that they enhance his narratives and were intended to do so. Fleming, he notes, does not interrupt vital action in the middle—a fatal writing flaw—but rather lingers to describe the already known, and to do so suggestively. On the first point, Eco notes that the elaborated descriptions are of card games, automobiles, airplane instrument panels, railway carriages, restaurant menus, a box of commonly available cigarettes. These are, to Eco's mind, already known objects; but, he argues, Fleming spends little time on the assault on Fort Knox because none of his readers will "ever have occasion to rob Fort Knox" (p. 67). "We identify ourselves not with the one who steals an atom bomb but with the one who steers a luxurious motor-launch; not with the one who explodes a rocket but with the one who accomplishes a lengthy ski descent" (pp. 67–68).

It seems to us, however, that this defense is an attempt—and a facile one at that—to make a virtue of Fleming's failures. Aimlessness and the extraneous have never been recognized virtues in writing; they do not seem to have gained adherents since Fleming. Eco's categories are questionable; the airplane's cockpit instrumentation is supposed to be "common"; but is it? Do we really identify with those who steer motor-launches, or make lengthy ski descents? Is a detailed knowledge of these activities requisite for understanding and appreciating Fleming? Precisely because the theft of an atom bomb is unfamiliar to us—as is an assault on Fort Knox—we want our imagination stimulated by the writer so that we will have confidence in what he is telling us. We want to believe that such improbable events could happen (or else the story is truly ridiculous), and it is the author's job to induce us to believe. Not to describe such unlikely and improbable events is an outright abdication of the mission of the writer, especially a writer who so commonly builds his plots around improbable actions.

Kingsley Amis had identified, and loudly praises, what he and others after him call the "Fleming effect." When the action in the story stagnates (Lilli, in Eco, pp. 158–59), Fleming "makes the action progress in an atmosphere that is itself moved in turn"—in trains, on motorcycles, etc. "Mechanized travel is so deeply built into our day-to-day habit that to swing the reader every time into participation testifies to a certain power of freshness." Amis puts the matter in an

aphorism: "the contemporary becomes romantic . . . the merely romantic solidly contemporary."

Aside from Amis and Eco, few critics are favorably disposed toward
Fleming's writing. Laura Lilli has summarized several of them in her
useful essay on "James Bond and Criticism" (in Eco, 1966, p. 157 ff.).
The novelist Alberto Moravia thought that from a literary point of view
Goldfinger "does not exist and would not be worth the trouble of discussing," the only point of Fleming's books being their psychological
and sociological aspects. Alberto Arbasino is as decided: "They are
badly written books, to say the least." Their structures are "rough-and-
ready," though he did find that "they are full of accessories that glit-
ter." Enzo Golino agrees. The Bond novels are "badly written, one
banality after another drawn from the most false and stereotyped language and flanked suddenly with wild inventions." He agrees with
Moravia that "these books attract the sociological eye more than the
literary *animus*."

Can we, from this welter of evidence, semifact, impression, and
emotion, infer some of the reasons for Bond's popularity? We want to
put aside for the present his influence with influential people. Many
of his fans did not know or care that JFK claimed to be an avid reader.
And we will also set aside the fact of his influence with publishers;
once his books had been published, readers were not forced to buy
them. Something in them spoke to millions. The movies were unquestionably crucial in developing the universal popularity of James
Bond, and their role should not be underestimated. But the movies do
not explain everything. *Doctor No,* the first movie released (*Casino Royale* was made earlier, but released later), was taken from Fleming's sixth
novel. The novels had been selling moderately well before the Connery
phenomenon. Something in the books themselves appealed to readers;
the millions of readers who bought books after they had seen the films
presumably enjoyed reading them.

Fleming's books can be enjoyed for their surface qualities alone.
They are "easy reads." Fleming's narratives are enjoyable because they
lack the complications and sophistication, the structural and stylistic
intricacies of much modern fiction. Not even the spy novels of John
Le Carré, Len Deighton, or Robert Littell are as "easy." Simple plots,
facile prose, easy reading. As some critics have claimed, Fleming wrote

updated fairy tales, stories known (though not always correctly) for their simplicity. He successfully captured the spirit of those authors of his youth, Yates, Buchan, and Sapper. Ours, a more sensitive generation, recoil at their (and Fleming's) sexism, racism, and chauvinism; but for a certain class of English readers, Bond was merely, and admirably, upholding the supremacy of the British race. He is also the champion and the embodiment of the upwardly mobile and their values; today, in America, we would expect Bond to drive a BMW. Finally—though by no means least important—Fleming told adventure stories in which the hero, the embodiment of most of the "right" values, inevitably triumphed. Fleming was right in his estimate: the public wanted old-fashioned, admirable heroes.

How seriously should we take the world of James Bond? Not very, if we are to believe those critics who see in his exaggerated improbabilities more than a touch of irony, or who, like John Cawelti, find Fleming's tongue in his cheek once or twice a page. If he is not to be taken seriously, what should be our response? Should we view the entire Bond corpus at arm's length because neither its world nor the inhabitants of its world were meant to be taken for "real"?

We know that the Broccoli/Saltzman movies were from the first ironic; they have been occasionally condemned for being spoofs played too broadly. As more Bond films appeared, elements of the fantastic and of the self-parodic became more pronounced. By the last Roger Moore characterizations, little believability remained. But these movies, though based on the books, are not the Bond books themselves.

In literary irony, the reader has an understanding with the author that the narrator is in some way untrustworthy (Booth, 1975, pp. 300 ff.)—humorous, or disgraceful, or ridiculous, or vicious. We do not believe that Fleming was a careful enough craftsman to make that subtle distinction between author and narrator, to separate himself from his created character of James Bond and the world that he had devised for him. We get no clues from the author that he was anything but serious about his hero's character and adventures. In fact, we believe that Fleming's identification with Bond was quite close, that the fictional secret agent bore many of his creator's character traits, that some of his exploits (with women, with the adventurous life) were projections of Fleming's desires. The novels were quickly written—in two months usually—and as quickly revised; Fleming did not have the time, if that was ever his intention, to carefully create a character or an implied author who would be the subject of his irony.

As Wayne Booth aptly remarks, "the reader's problem is that of discriminating between genuinely functional difficulty and obscurities that spring from carelessness, false pride, or plain ineptitude" (p. 303). Regarding Fleming, we do not feel that we are in collusion with the author or that we are given information that would lead us to view the protagonist with irony. Irony, Booth points out, requires that the protagonist's view of his own actions (whether conveyed in first-person or third-person narration) be counterpointed against an opposite view that the character's words and action reveal to the reader (p. 305); he was talking of "classical drama," but the same principle holds for the novel. What do characters in the Bond cycle say or do that would lead us to suspect there is something amiss with 007?

Such clues are not there. Aware that irony is one of the easiest qualities to read into a text, we must conclude that Cawelti's interpretation of the ironic Fleming is a case of a sensitive and intelligent reader confronting a casual writer, and making the best of the text. We can contrast Fleming with Robert Littell, a spy novelist and a skillful handler of irony. Almost any one of Littell's novels will serve to illustrate this quality well, but especially *The Sisters*. The author conspires with the reader without a word passing between them; but sufficient nudges and pokes get the point across. Littell is able to accomplish this without sacrificing characterization (even some of the KGB agents are congenial), and the plot is as tightly structured as one finds in the genre, with frequent switchbacks that truly fit Aristotle's description of "reversal." Next to such a writer (and Littell is by no means one of the great novelists writing today in English), Fleming's work is pale, his putative irony imperceptible.

From our biographical perspective, it is tempting to see in Fleming a good deal of irony, particularly self-irony; we know that publicly (but only in the first few years of his career) he occasionally deprecated his own imaginative stories. With James Bond as something of a success, Fleming could denounce him as that "cardboard booby." That is part of the Etonian gentleman syndrome. The true aristocrat, who could do anything with ease, must not take his writing too seriously. In fact (as Pearson observes, pp. 190–91), *Casino Royale* was written with amazing—and thus seemingly effortless—ease and speed. For Fleming to do it right, the Bond books had to be at least modestly successful; otherwise, the impact of his having written them effortlessly loses its force. If there is irony, then, it is concealed in some private joke he enjoyed exclusively with himself and that he played continually on his readers. For Fleming, the only irony lay in that deeply personal ironic distance between the author's innermost feelings and his public stance. That irony—which is not part of the novels but rather a fact of the author's psychology—we can acknowledge, and perhaps pity.

Chapter Five
Live Sources, Paper Imitations

James Bond was, as we have seen, created by Ian Fleming in the heroic mode in an ironic age. Bond defeats his enemies—Dr. No, Goldfinger, Mr. Big, Blofeld; but John Le Carré's Alec Leamas is shot down while escaping over the Berlin Wall. Bond is the seducer of many beautiful women, all of whom are devoted to him only; Le Carré's George Smiley loses his wife for a time to a Cuban race-car driver, and Bernie Samson's wife turns out to have been a KGB officer all along, exploiting him for secret information. Bond's natural sexual vitality persuades lesbian Pussy Galore into his bed; Len Deighton's hero in *Spy Story* falls in love with a woman who turns out not only to be another secret agent but also a lesbian, and so their romance brusquely ends. Bond survives because he endures pain, and he conquers his adversary because of the mistakes, usually prideful, of his diabolical adversary; Smiley unearths the mole in the Secret Service and then forces the defection of his Russian counterpart, Karla, through intellect and cunning and brilliant detective work. Bond is sent on missions by his father/God figure, "M," an embodiment of Establishment England; the agent Harry Palmer in Len Deighton's *The Ipcress File,* some of Smiley's people, and the agent in *Assignment K* are all betrayed by their superior officers, who are actually undercover Russian agents. Bond's enemies are always "over there"; the enemy in most other contemporary spy fiction is everywhere.

Yet, despite these anachronisms, Fleming knew, or knew of, several people whose life-styles fit the template he had chosen—or perhaps provided a model for that template. Bond's literary predecessors appear in the boy's fiction of Yates, Buchan, and Sapper, perhaps even the "Raffles" novels; we also know that many of Bond's attitudes and reflexes are Fleming's own, projected without much camouflaging. People Fleming knew, or knew of and had heard stories and anecdotes about, had led adventurous, flamboyant lives; their escapades shaped Fleming's conception of his master spy. Since these people were real and had done the things everyone knew they had done, reasoned Fleming, James Bond must be a believable character. Two men in particular were living paradigms of the heroic-mold secret agent: Sidney Reilly and the double agent Dusko Popov who was code-named "Tricycle." They were clandestine operatives whom Fleming, because of his Intelligence work during the war and his several knowledgeable friends, knew about. He may even have met Tricycle.

As an often-quoted anecdote has it, when Robin Bruce Lockhart, author of *Reilly: Ace of Spies,* called Fleming to congratulate him on the publication of *Casino Royale,* the inventor of James Bond responded that his hero "is just a piece of nonsense I dreamed up. He's not a Sidney Reilly, you know" (Lockhart, 1984, p. 11). That famous legend of espionage work is said to have died on a clandestine mission in Russia in 1925.

This story, first related orally and later fixed in print, implies several relationships that are relevant here. First, Lockhart was on more than nodding terms with Fleming, or he would not have made such a congratulatory call. During World War II he worked for Naval Intelligence Division, and it was at the admiralty that he first met Ian Fleming (Lockhart, 1984, p. 9). Fleming, in his turn, of course knew of Lockhart's connection with and abiding interest in Reilly; Lockhart's father, Sir Robert Bruce Lockhart, had served with Reilly in Russia around the time of the Revolution and had conspired with him to overthrow—or at least to undermine—the Bolshevik cause. This is now known in Russia as "The Lockhart Plot," though the son insists that owing to Reilly's role as mastermind of it, the conspiracy should be known as "The Reilly Plot" (Lockhart, *First Man,* p. 1).

Since the son's popular book, *Reilly: Ace of Spies,* had not yet been published, Fleming's knowledge of the Lockhart/Reilly connection had to be based on orally transmitted stories. The circle in which such stories circulated would have included novelist W. Somerset Maugham, a British Secret Service agent in Moscow at the time of the Bolshevik Revolution, and later a friend of Fleming and his wife. Certainly stories about Reilly, his spectacular espionage successes, and his presumed death in Russia in 1925 were current among army and naval Intelligence officers. Fleming, sociable in his wartime days and highly placed, had access to many stories about the legendary ace of spies. Donald McCormick (Richard Deacon) knew Fleming personally; he was assistant foreign manager under him when they both worked for the Kemsley empire. He tells us that "almost certainly" Fleming would have heard stories about Reilly first when he disappeared in 1925, in the press and through his brother, Peter. Then, McCormick thinks, Fleming would have heard more about this legend of espionage when he was in Russia as a reporter for Reuters in the early 1930s. What he heard while personal assistant for the DNI would have added to his stock of Reilly stories; by that time he would have been quite familiar with the agent's life.

Fleming would have us believe that between missions the life of James Bond was quite boring; from what is known of Reilly, he was never bored, because he was almost never between assignments. Reilly was a notoriously flamboyant high-lifer and a prodigious womanizer; his biographer, Michael Kettle, called him "A gay lothario who loved parties" (p. 18). Reilly was the illegitimate son of a Russian Jewish mother and her lover; his real name was probably Sigmund Rosenblum. He claimed that his father was an Irish sea captain, hence the Irish family name (Knightley, p. 58). Reilly was able to pull off some spectacular espionage successes; when he failed, even the attempt was magnificent. But he was not exclusively an establishment operative as spies are commonly thought to be; often he acted on his own initiative in what he felt were his own best interests, regardless of orders or his employer's wishes. He was an espionage entrepreneur, often a free-lance agent, though most often in the employ of the British government.

When the Russo-Japanese War began, he was in Port Arthur as the chief agent of the Compagnie Est-Asiatique. He probably used inside information to buy up stores of certain necessary materials and then sold them to the combatants at a handsome profit. James Bond would not have involved himself in such tawdry business, no matter how imaginative—unless it were on behalf of king and country and honor.

Lockhart credits Reilly with securing oil and mineral rights in Persia for the British (p. 44 ff.). Learning that the mining engineer D'Arcy was negotiating with the Rothschilds for the rights to Persian oil, Reilly disguised himself as a priest and innocently boarded Rothschild's yacht. Once aboard, he managed to get D'Arcy alone and told him that the British government would pay him double the price offered by the French. England got the concession. This is more like the James Bond style and panache. With it came millions of pounds in profit and access to all the petroleum that England's industry—especially its military and naval operations—would need. The company formed is today's BP.

Several years later, employed by Russian naval contractors in Petrograd who were charged with rebuilding the navy after the war, Reilly secretly negotiated with Blohm and Voss, German shipbuilders, giving them inside bidding information. He made a personal fortune from the German company's commissions. This activity has been applauded by the British because Reilly was, at the same time, able to give the admiralty a tremendous amount of technical information about German naval armaments—everything, in fact, that he had access to at Blohm and Voss.

Reilly's greatest audacious act was still to come. He probably knew, with an insider's knowledge, about the Zinoviev letter. This letter, allegedly written by the president of the Communist International in mid-September 1924, advised members of the British Communist party to arm themselves for a revolution in Britain, intensifying their work both within the armed forces and within the Labor party. Leaked to the press a few days before a general election in 1924, it is credited with costing the Labor party the election. The letter's publicity also finished off any chances for the proposed Anglo-Russian trade treaty then being considered by the government and damaged relations between England and Russia for decades (Knightley, p. 62). The letter was subsequently revealed to have been a forgery, probably brought to the attention of SIS by Sidney Reilly. But when it first came to light, the Foreign Office's examination suggested that it was genuine, and several interested and politically motivated cabals maneuvered to get the letter into the hands of the press. Once public, the plot was irretrievable, and the damage could never be entirely undone. "There is little doubt," says Knightley (p. 63), "that Reilly had a hand in the affair."

Years earlier, when the Bolsheviks had stormed the Winter Palace, Reilly happened to be in Russia, established as a Soviet government official with access to official foreign ministry documents (Knightley, pp. 58–59). Based on what he saw in the foreign ministry and in the streets, he decided that the Bolsheviks were an even greater enemy than Germany, "a hideous cancer striking at the very root of civilisation" (quoted in Knightley, p. 59). His scheme for the overthrow of the Bolsheviks—variously known as "The Lettish Plot" or "The Lockhart Plot"—would have subverted the Latvian troops who were the bodyguards of the Bolshevik leaders. As Reilly had planned it, the Latvians would arrest Lenin and Trotsky, while Reilly and his followers would establish a provisional government. An important part of the scheme involved the assassination of Lenin by one of Reilly's accomplices, Dora Kaplan.

She did her part—almost. She got two shots off at Lenin, striking him twice, but she failed to kill him. Reilly always insisted that he was within a hair of toppling the Soviets, but, in the event, it was a spectacular failure. The Latvian guards never changed sides, and with his plot in cinders Reilly fled the country. Back in England he took on the Bolsheviks almost as a personal cause. He began visiting VIPs to warn them of the danger of bolshevism. He involved himself deeply in White Russian politics and participated in and supported many of their counter-revolutionary plans. At the same time he traveled extensively in England and the United States to raise money with which to fight the new enemy. When he was informed about an anti-Soviet organization within Russia known as "The Trust," he decided that it would be the best way to bring down the Soviets; in order to liaise with and lend this group his support he returned to Russia, incognito—or so he thought. He was never heard from again in the West. He was probably captured by the Russian secret police or by CHEKA (forerunner of the KGB) and subsequently killed.

It is characteristic of this man more than of most secret agents that mystery shrouds his death. One version of his end has it that The Trust was a front for the secret police, established to lure right-wing money into Russian hands, and that Reilly, who had told Trust members of his return, was almost immediately captured and executed (Knightley, p. 59). Another has it that he escaped, went underground, and continued to fight against the Bolsheviks until he died of old age. This last legend has the quality of "the hero too noble and clever to be dead" about it; variants of it exist about Charlemagne, JFK, Che Guevera, even Hitler who for decades was supposedly "alive and well in Argentina." A third possibility has surfaced, in Robin Bruce Lockhart's most recent book, *Reilly: The First Man*. This interpretation has Reilly joining CHEKA (he was, after all, Russian born, and the pull of the motherland was not to be resisted) and plotting the infiltration of British Intelligence. Reilly thus becomes the agent who recruited Philby, Maclean, Burgess, and Blunt.

Even though no Bond novel or episode is based on any one of Reilly's adventures, the magnitude of Reilly's actions and the flamboyance of his personal life duplicated in their audacity the imaginative capers that Fleming had given to 007. Bond had an independent income; Reilly had to earn his, however unethical the dealings, though in time he amassed a comfortable hoard. Boarding Rothschild's yacht in disguise in order to speak privately with one of the guests has an imaginative audacity worthy of Bond. So, too, has the idea of a plot to overthrow the Bolsheviks and to take Russia's destiny in one's own hands. But it was Reilly's life-style as much as anything that must have convinced Fleming that the fantastic, glittering life he imagined for James Bond had been lived by real people. Lockhart's biography (p. 27 ff.) has the young "Sidney" (which Reilly early changed from Sigmund) ever fastidious about his clothes, spending liberally at tailors and shirtmakers. He dined at fashionable restaurants and frequented casinos, playing for high stakes, and often winning. While still a young man he is said to have had a tempestuous affair with a prostitute; like Fleming he had many lovers, but unlike the Englishman he married more than once—three times as a matter of fact.

Fleming began collecting the books "that made a difference" as a young man. And Reilly also, while touring Elba with an early love, became fascinated with Napoleon and (so Lockhart has it, p. 29) "the seeds of a burning and ruthless ambition were sown." Reilly began an extensive collection of Napoleonic souvenirs and relics, but to pay for this newfound obsession and the life-style he thoroughly relished and the women he wished to court, he needed money. Clothes, Napoleoniana, and card-playing consumed nearly all of his money. Lockhart calls gambling "his one vice" (Lockhart, pp. 35, 60); apparently bigamy, adultery, lying, betraying confidences, and unethical business practices were acceptable.

Ever the free-wheeler, in the espionage game for his own profit, Sidney Reilly was a spy with his own personal foreign policy. Other spies have had their likes and dislikes regarding foreign policy and international political matters, but Reilly was one of the few who had the ability to carry out his inclinations. Fleming was right: Bond was not really a Sidney Reilly, perhaps because Reilly's adventures would seem to be too improbable to be related in print. Fleming wanted a hero, but one a little more ordinary.

During the war, when Fleming and Admiral Godfrey stopped over in Lisbon on their flight to Washington, another spy—also known for his flamboyant life-style—claims to have been at the casino on the same night. It seems to have been a more notable occasion than Fleming realized at the time, or when he used the episode—if he did—in *Casino Royale*. A young Yugoslav, Dusko Popov—a double agent working for MI 5 as one of their Double XX operatives, though ostensibly working for the German secret service, the *Abwehr*—has said that he and Fleming did "rub shoulders" that night (quoted in McCormick, p. 92).

Popov, known more widely by his wartime code name Tricycle, was carrying $80,000 in cash, which the Germans had just given him to keep financing the spy ring he was supposed to be controlling in Britain. Since he was not to turn the money over to MI 6 officers until the next day, he carried the cash with him. Out of boredom he visited the casino at Estoril. He says that he had observed Fleming following him all evening—at a café before dinner, at the restaurant, then at the casino. Tricycle's conclusion was that Fleming was acting on his own, since he felt certain that MI 6 trusted him with money; as he put it, the information in his head was worth far more than that. But where was Godfrey at this time, if Fleming was, as Tricycle claims, following him on his own? Fleming's version has him and the DNI going to the casino together out of boredom; Popov depicts a fairly active, though inept, shadow. Had Fleming really "got wind" of the operation that involved Tricycle carrying around $80,000 for more than twenty-four hours, as the Yugoslav claimed?

In any event, Tricycle found at the Chemin de fer tables a man he did not especially like, a wealthy Lithuanian named Bloch, and on a reckless whim decided to embarrass him. Tricycle opened the betting at $50,000, and when the Lithuanian could not match this bet—who carries that kind of money around?—Fleming's "face turned bile green" (p. 92). The moment was Popov's, in his narrative at least. Turning to the croupier, he said that he assumed that the house would back the Lithuanian's bet. When told, as he fully expected, that the house never backed individual gamblers, Tricycle announced triumphantly that he assumed that in the future "such irresponsible play will be prohibited" (p. 93).

Recruited into the *Abwehr* in the summer of 1940 (West, 1982, p. 197 ff.), Popov immediately reported the operation to the Belgrade SIS agent, then operating under the cover of a passport control officer. MI5 in London decided to use him as a double agent, and he was consequently instructed to go along with all of the *Abwehr*'s plans. One of Popov's most important missions for the Germans was the establishment of a spy ring in Britain; Popov, at first code-named "Scout" but shortly after "Tricycle" by MI 5 (because he had just "tripled" his value [West, p. 198]), did set up such a ring, all of whose members were loyal to Britain. Throughout the war—Tricycle operated for about three and a half years, an unusually long time for a secret agent—a great deal of correct trivia and false information was fed back to Germany. Sent by the Germans to the United States in 1941—the trip on which he stopped in Lisbon—he feuded with J. Edgar Hoover and, after what the staid Nigel West described as "twelve months of womanising and night clubbing at the expense of BSC" (West, p. 200), was brought back to Lisbon.

He was nothing if not audacious; in Portugal's capital he convinced his contact in the *Abwehr* that his failure to establish operating rings had been largely their fault for not giving him enough money. His excuse was believed, and a week later he returned to Britain (on German orders this time) with several thousand dollars and a new assignment. Despite his playboy persona Tricycle was an effective agent. He kept his true mission secret even from people who worked for him. His radio operator ("Freak," the code name for the Marquis de Ruda) did not know of many of the content of the messages he was sending (West, p. 205), but the Germans were satisfied by the volume of relatively high-level information they received. The network was kept active until the imminent invasion of France in June 1944 put an end to its usefulness.

Fleming, we have seen, needed no model for James Bond beyond his own reading and especially his own life—inner and projected—but if he needed reassurance that such personal flamboyance, such panache could be found in the real world, he had the examples of Sidney Reilly and of Tricycle. Whatever Tricycle's true loyalty, whatever Reilly's effectiveness (or his true loyalty, for that matter), they were audacious men whose conspicuous actions made them the subject of many anecdotes. They became legends while they still lived. Both wrote autobiographies—*The Adventures of Sidney Reilly* and *Spy Counterspy*—that certainly helped spread stories of their exploits, and so further enhanced their fame. Both men—if we do not question their lives or their values too closely—were just the sort of stuff that Ian Fleming had in mind for his hero. Bond was to be as flamboyant as Reilly or Tricycle, perhaps—he was to be a gentleman after all—but, as a secret agent, he was to be cut from the same cloth.

Ultimately, of course, the material for the life and character of James Bond came from Fleming's own life. The novels are projections of aspects of his inner life, of which he was probably unconscious, as well as depictions of his conscious aspirations, attitudes, and life-style. The lives of Reilly and Popov exerted less influence on the content of the James Bond novels, and their contribution was somewhat indirect.

Bond, like Reilly, was at home with the world's intrigues. Like Tricycle, he was a womanizer and high-living bon vivant. Fleming

wanted his books to be successful, in part so that he could live a gentleman's comfortable life in Jamaica. Fictional character, real spy, adventurer, and double agent: Fleming drew on all of them and his own
imagination to the benefit of James Bond.

Given to violence and unashamed of cruelty, this new hero of the
1950s and 1960s was what the public wanted. Certainly, it responded
to him. The violence of our time has made the violence of James Bond
and his imitators acceptable. And because few members of his public
had access to "the finer things" of life but many aspired to them, the
life-style of Bond—like that of Reilly and Popov—had enormous appeal. Take Fleming's focus on brand names, for instance. A journalist's
device for engaging his reader, it also enabled him to present a set of
meaningful allusions. For a consumption-oriented readership, a Bentley, Beluga caviar, Savile Row tailors and Dom perignon '46 had
meaning. These artifacts invoked a fantasy world. For an audience obsessed with things, things take on a reverberating significance of their
own, and the invocation of things has associative meanings. Whether
Fleming saw that deeply into contemporary life or whether his method
manifested what he felt about objects himself, he used the evocative
power of brand names as no writer before him ever had done. He made
Bond a man of his time.

And he made James Bond a man of his time in other respects as
well. Although Fleming never succeeded in making Bond a convincing
bureaucrat, he insisted that such was his intention. In any event, 007
is the first major fictional spy to operate out of an espionage agency,
an organization with secretaries, chiefs of staff, armorers, and a director
with a personality. Nearly all of these characters were creative failures,
or so the critics thought. But Fleming's idea of the spy as organization
man (he is, after all, officially a man with a number, 007), however
faultily executed, made Bond a "modern" spy. Later, Deighton and Le
Carré and Hall and Littell would do the job better, but Fleming was
first. His muse was not entirely asleep. Fleming had some vision.
Bond's violence, amoral sexuality, pretentiousness, and aggressive het-
erosexuality have diverted us from an appreciation of Fleming's ability
to embrace much that is modern in modern life.

Bond continues not only the tradition of the American hard-boiled
detective, like Philip Marlowe and Sam Spade, but also the tradition
of man in modernist literature. As Fausto Antonini has put it (in Eco,
p. 108 ff.), Bond is cold, detached, distant, hard, severe, implacably

cruel, "the archetype of . . . a hero imagined and produced by the collective unconscious contemporary psyche." His legalized permission to kill gratifies modern man, beset with countless restrictions and prohibitions, continually thwarted in his desire to do as he wants. Bond is without interior dimensions, without history, creativity, or philosophical curiosity. He is a creature of adventure and action, of calculation and erotic emotion. Thus Bond "saves" the reader from his/her own insecurity, inferiority, and fear—from a sense of guilt and from the effort of thinking. The "detached irony" (p. 120) that shows itself in Bond's weltanschauung is, Antonini thinks, Ian Fleming's message to the world.

Hard-boiled, unintellectual, opinionated about a few material concerns, there is much of us in this cardboard booby. Fleming's readers have been willing to pay to read about a hero who does all the "right" things in "a radically simplified but still recognizable version of [his] own oppressively unsimple world" (Van Dover, p. 13). For the plodders, working at routine nine-to-five jobs, Bond's life has meaning. Wish fulfillment or fearful fantasy, Bond became a man for the 1960s. The continued success of the 007 movies and the continuation of the fiction by John Gardner demonstrates that he is still current—a man for this season.

So enormous was the impact of James Bond that a flock of other spy novelists, not all of whom were yet actively writing at the time, determined either to imitate him or to create spies who would correct the impressions left by what they felt were Fleming's excesses. Members of espionage agencies knew that Fleming's plots and characters bore almost no resemblance to their lives or those of the people who inhabit the shadow world. But the public, who had little understanding of spying in the twentieth century, could not be certain. It was to reach the public, to correct exaggerated impressions, and to satisfy their own selves about the truth of the matter that many writers turned to writing spy novels. Antagonists and imitators: Fleming's writing launched dozens of careers.

John Le Carré, writer of some of the most successful—and, more important, some of the best—spy novels since World War II, is one of the hostiles. Recently he talked to a seminar at Johns Hopkins University about his life and his writing (reported in *The Johns Hopkins Magazine,* August 1986, pp. 11–16), commenting that his knowledge of espionage came from having served for several years first in Army Intelligence and later with the Foreign Office. The hero of several of his recent books is George Smiley, who has a bit of the author in his makeup:

. . . without giving the matter much thought, [I] began writing about a man called George Smiley, putting him together from various components—either real or imagined—of my own situation, and adding the solvent of my own filial affection and admiration.

Smiley was shy, as I tended to be, and had difficulty walking into a crowded room.

He was anonymous, as I was, and by choice as well as professional necessity self-effacing.

But there was more to Smiley than his role as a Le Carré manqué, for his creator also had Ian Fleming somewhere in the back of his mind:

If his tastes differed in every way that I can think of from those of James Bond, as did his sex life, he was still, ultimately, the reluctant servant of established Western society: even if Western society in its institutional forms presented itself to him as unfeeling, decadent, and self-serving. Somewhere in Smiley's search—beyond all the dross and disenchantment of an ever more materialistic world—the romantic blue flower beckoned to him, and he plodded after it. (p. 15)

James Bond is about six feet tall, muscular and athletic, in his mid-thirties, scarred on his right cheek, one comma of his black hair falling over his right eyebrow. His gray-blue eyes and his mouth hold a hint of cruelty. Like Fleming, Bond went to Eton for a short time, but was dismissed for unseemly extra-curricular activities; like Fleming, he then went to the University of Geneva; and again, like Fleming, he was happiest in Kitzbuhel, where he learned to ski. Smiley is also a professional Intelligence officer, but there the similarity with Bond ends. He is a middle-aged scholar of German literature whose love of his subject was strained by his World War II experiences. He is, as Le Carré imagined him, "tubby and perplexed, the weary pilgrim is struggling up a stony hill, carrying his exhausted horse on his shoulders" (p. 15). In *Call for the Dead* (1961) he is described in the chapter "A Brief History of George Smiley" in this way: "Short, fat and of a quiet disposition, he appeared to spend a lot of money on really bad clothes, which hung about his squat frame like a skin on a shrunken toad" (p. 7). An acquaintance of his wife's quips about the wedding that the bride "was mated to a bullfrog in a sou'wester" (p. 7). Readers and viewers nevertheless (or because of these qualities?) find him congenially admirable. Those who encounter him casually in Le Carré's pages have identified with "a little, fat man, rather gloomy," sometimes mistaken for a tired executive "out for a bit of fun" (p. 189).

The Spy Who Came in from the Cold (1963) was Le Carré's first important novel, and is still used as a standard by which good espionage fiction is judged. It was probably motivated largely by the author's dislike of the Bond novels. Fleming's hero went to Eton for a spell, enjoyed the good (i.e., expensive) things of the world of the upwardly mobile classes, often drove a Bentley or an Aston-Martin, seduced nearly all of the desirable women he encountered. Le Carré actually taught at Eton for a brief spell (about the only connection he had with Fleming's world); he was a tutor in French and German. His Alec Leamas has become the model of the unheroic spy. Leamas hates Americans and public schools; when he is back in London he takes the public bus; he drinks beer, not the "right" wines and champagnes and vodka martinis; and his one affair is with a lonely, not attractive, librarian whom he genuinely cares for.

Fleming was the first important writer to place his hero within a bureaucratic espionage agency, but it was Le Carré who described how perfidious and self-serving such agencies could be. Le Carré (in Mc-Cormack, 1979, p. 132) vehemently denounced Fleming's spy: "the really interesting thing about Bond is that he would be what I would call the ideal defector. Because if the money was better, the booze freer and women easier over there in Moscow, he'd be off like a shot. Bond, you see, is the ultimate prostitute." By contrast, Smiley and Leamas are men of integrity and conscience. Le Carré made them believable, and he made them sympathetic. Most importantly, he gave a respectability to espionage fiction, a quality that Fleming had compromised with his brand-name-dropping, libidinally hyperactive hero, his evil fairy-tale villains, and his science fiction plots. Le Carré, more than any writer except Graham Greene, brought the modern spy novel into the mainstream of modern fiction.

That John Gardner wrote some of his early novels as a reaction to the character of James Bond has to be seen as one of life's ironies. The son of a clergyman, Gardner served in the military in the Far East; went to St. Johns, Cambridge, where he earned a degree in theology;

was ordained and spent five years as a clergyman; and subsequently spurned the cloth to become a journalist. After a spy novel writing career based on a dislike for James Bond, he was selected by Fleming's estate executors to continue the James Bond cycle. He has written several Bond novels in the past few years.

Unlike Le Carré, Gardner had no personal experience with any Intelligence service. But for the kind of novel he wrote he hardly needed any. The focal character of the first adventure/spy novels is the anti-Bond antihero Boysie Oakes. Gardner's spy is a lot like George Smiley: over forty years old, he is prone to airsickness, acrophobic, and fearful of violence. His author has described him as "the picture of what most of us are like—luxury-loving, lecherous, and a mass of neuroses" (in McCormick, p. 103). Like Bond, Oakes is something of a Don Juan, but unlike Bond his efforts are marked by a rather severe moral code, thickly coated with guilt. He has been known to break off a seduction attempt because he decides mid-stream that it isn't "nice." His job in the secret service is to assassinate British agents thought by their superiors to be security risks. But instead of doing the jobs himself—he is really quite a docile person—he subcontracts his assignments out to gangster friends.

The Liquidator (1964), introducing Boysie Oakes, was a great success in England. With its sharp wit and comedic situations, as well as some exciting scenes, this anti-Fleming, anti-Bond parody entertained a large readership, larger (McCormick estimates) than that of Le Carré's early books. If Fleming's books were a kind of science fiction (whose ironies, if any, were undetected by a majority of English audiences), and Le Carré's were tense dramas that struck the reader with the impact of a clenched fist, Gardner's provided the comic relief. And their light demythologizing tone had great appeal, both in novel form and shortly after as a film. *Amber Nine* (1966), *Madrigal* (1967), *Founder Member* (1969), *The Airline Pirates* (1970), *Traitor's Exit* (1970), and *Understrike* (1973) continued the adventures of Boysie Oakes. But in recent years—irony of ironies—Oakes has been replaced in Gardner's thoughts, and put in his out-basket, by his original nemesis: James Bond.

The imitations of Bond are several. Donald Hamilton's Matt Helm is the most clearly derivative. In the movies Matt is played, suavely, ironically, sophisticatedly, by Dean Martin—not Sean Connery, exactly, but close enough by the standards of American "B" movies.

Adam Hall, the creator of secret agent Quiller, was—like Fleming—
fascinated by guns:

> All the Husqvarnas are beautiful but the finest they make is the 561. It is a
> .358 Magnum center-fire, with a three-shot magazine, 25½ inch barrel,
> hand-checkered walnut stock, corrugated butt-plate and sling-swivels. The
> fore-end and pistol grip are tipped with rosewood. The total weight is 7 ¾
> pounds and the breech pressure is in the region of 20 tons p.s.i., giving a
> high muzzle velocity and an almost flat trajectory with a 150-grain bul-
> let. . . . I had chosen an exemplary Balvar 6 by Bausch and Lomb with an
> optical variable from X 2½ to X 5. Its feature is that as the magnification
> power is increased the crosshair reticle remains constant in size and does not
> therefore tend to obscure the target. (p. 74)

British novelist Kingsley Amis is an enthusiastic Fleming fan. After
Fleming's death, Amis wrote a spy story on his own—*Colonel Sun*
(1968)—which never achieved much popularity. Another follower is
Trevanian, whose violence has achieved some success on this side of the
Atlantic—with little subtlety. Trevanian's characters are named in the
Fleming mode: Ms. Arce, Jonathan Hemlock, Wormwood, Eurasis
Dragon, Anna Bidet, and Randie Nickers. Rather obvious, but then
so was Honeychile Rider and Pussy Galore.

Not even Fleming's plots are safe. Alistair Maclean's *The Black Shrike*
(1961) is obviously indebted to *Doctor No* (1958). In Maclean's narrative, the hero (John Bentall) and his woman (Marie Hopeman, who,
in the best Fleming tradition, is shapely and attractive) escape from a
schooner on which they have been ostensibly kidnapped and drift to a
coral atoll in the South Pacific. At this point in the story the similarity
with *Doctor No* becomes evident. Maclean's island, like Fleming's, is
rich in guano; gathering it is the ostensible reason for its being occupied. A demonic master criminal on the island (like Dr. No) has killed
the local archaeologist and taken on a disguise meant to fool the un-
wary into thinking that he is the scientist. MacLean's villain plans to
take over a Royal Navy missile base located at the other end of the
island, Vardu; Dr. No's scheme is to divert American missiles elec-
tronically while in flight. Fleming went on to use a similar plot as the
basis of *Thunderball*.

The demon of Vardu, LeClerc, plans to use his captured missiles—
the "Black Shrikes" of the book's title—in the service of China (remi-
niscent of the Chinese Negroes in *Doctor No*) to subdue both Russia

and the United States. Unlike Bond, MacLean's Bentall is very clever, but like Bond he endures great pain while attempting to discover the fiend's plot. Maclean devotes a good deal of space to the technical aspects of the firing of the missiles: Bentall, like Bond, is expert in some aspects of rocketry. LeClerc's oxine assistant, Hewell, seems to borrow his characterization from several fictional heavies. He can be seen as a variant of Oddjob, but he is also like any of dozens of other beefy henchman, not necessarily Fleming's. Bentall is glib in the hard-boiled tradition, though he falls victim to Marie's charms and actually proposes marriage to her. Unlike James Bond, Bentall blames himself for everything that goes wrong on his island adventure. In the end, however, he is successful. He overthrows LeClerc and exposes his administrative superior back in London as a double agent.

And Fleming's influence overspread not only espionage fiction and movies, but television as well. Patrick McGoohan, who turned down an early offer to play James Bond in film, emerged as John Drake in the popular television series "Secret Agent." McGoohan is alleged to have decided against the Bond role on moral grounds (Rubin, p. 14). Drake was coolly cerebral—very much the modernist man—who treated women as fellow humans, with no chronic designs upon their chastity. Although the "secret agent man," with "a number instead of a name" (as the program's theme song would have it), was not modeled on Fleming's hero, there is no doubt that Bond's emergence as a hero/spy had paved the way.

Other, more derivative, television adventure series include "The Man From U.N.C.L.E." One of the two leads in this consistently ironic production was actor Robert Vaughn's role as "Napoleon Solo," the name originating in Goldfinger's criminal guest list. Movie producers Broccoli and Saltzman brought self-parody and clear spoof elements to the novel's characters and to Bond's adventures—an aspect that Fleming may have tried to infuse in his later writing—and "The Man From U.N.C.L.E." capitalized on the popularity of this tonal point of view. From the popularity of this television program came the very lightweight pornographic fiction series, *The Man From L.U.S.T.* and *The Girl from B.U.S.T.*, second-generation spin-offs of Fleming's original. Those novels are no longer being written, and all are out of print. "The Man From U.N.C.L.E." and "Secret Agent" had their last performances decades ago; in 1987 actor Timothy Dalton and producer "Cubby" Broccoli continued the James Bond movie cycle with *The Living Daylights.*

If we were to speak of Fleming's lasting contributions to the genre of the espionage novel in general, the list would be brief though not entirely trivial. James Bond was a member of a compartmentalized governmental agency, probably the first spy/hero of fiction to be so situated. After Fleming there are hardly any fictional spies who are not bureaucrats, though all of them—Bernie Sampson, Charley Heller (Robert Littell's victimized agent/hero), Harry Palmer, Alec Leamas, Charlie Muffin (Brian Freemantle's protagonist), George Smiley—respond to their situations more actively and are able to criticize these organizations. Yet if Fleming had not thought of it, it is likely that some other writer would have hit upon this idea. The founding of spy agencies was at this time occurring all over the real world: the KGB, the CIA, MI 5 and MI 6, the FBI. But Fleming did have the idea first, and to him must go the credit.

Nevertheless, Fleming did not contribute very much to the genre of the spy novel. He was not a skilled craftsman in the handling of character or plot, and so he was not able to contribute much to the form. And though in his influence on other writers, negative as well as positive, his historical role has been enormous; his imitators—Donald Hamilton and the like—have not made big splashes. Features that others have taken over—Fleming's great interest in gadgets, especially his fascination with guns, his love of high living—have not been wholly transferable. Aspects of Fleming's writing style have been copied, but the personality of Fleming and the life-style of Bond have been harder to imitate. They are the author's hallmarks.

Those who were offended by Bond and who took up writing spy novels to correct what they considered Fleming's excesses are significant contributors to the genre. Le Carré and Deighton have defined the direction of the contemporary spy novel and have been the major forces in making it a socially significant genre. Le Carré has said of the alleged limiting influence of the spy novel: "I am pretty sure that I regard the spy novel not as a confinement, but as an all-weather friend who can go anywhere I can take him" (*Hopkins Magazine*, p. 13).

Whether hostile or admiring, writings of espionage fiction in the last two decades have been greatly influenced by the character of James Bond and by the kind of fiction that Fleming wrote. We cannot credit Fleming with "inspiring" Le Carré and Gardner in the usual sense. But if Fleming had been of little account and largely ignored, his antagonists would not have been so incensed as to write fiction surpassing that of their hostile muse. Other spy novelists might never have written at all, and still others would have written differently. The enemies of James Bond have shaped the modern spy novel, but we should not lose sight of Bond's influence in that shaping. And we should remember that more than the spy novel has been altered by Fleming's novels. He made his mark on our attitudes and our life-styles. By imposing on us his philosophy of life and his notorious hero, he has induced us to reflect, sometimes searchingly, on ourselves.

Chapter Six

James Bond and the Modern Spy Novel

The early critics of Fleming's novels did not think his writing good enough to comment on in depth; they thought that he was merely a "phenomenon," and that the only profitable critical perspective was sociological. We focus here only partly on James Bond's extraordinary popular success. Our main interest is in a related matter: the place of Bond the character and Fleming the author within the context of the spy novel tradition in England and America. Looking at this context, we can learn more from the Fleming phenomenon than we would from speculating about the extraordinary sales of his books. We can explore several important questions: What are the potentials of the genre for a description and evaluation of contemporary life? Did Fleming understand those expressive potentials? Where does the character of James Bond lie within the tradition of fictional spies? To what extent is Bond the symbol of the spy in the contemporary world?

The genre is not an old one, yet it has already gone through three identifiable phases: the heroic, the sinister, and the ironic. In the first of these, the hero (as often as not an amateur gentleman spy-catcher, not himself a spy) was cleverer and physically superior to his enemies. John Buchan's Richard Hannay is of this type; so are Somerset Maugham's Ashenden, and Sapper's Bulldog Drummond—though the last had no large intellect. Nearer to World War II, especially in the novels of Graham Greene and Eric Ambler, and resuming after that conflict (in a number of novels by lesser writers), came the sinister phase. The hero was as often as not a victim of the enemy's forces. His characteristic stance was to be on-the-run, in flight for his mission, even his life. John Le Carré introduced the third phase of espionage fiction, the ironic, in which the hero is victimized by his own agency, his own countrymen, by the people we would normally expect to protect him. (This idea was actually first explored in Greene's *The Confi-*

dential Agent [1939], but as an idea it was left undeveloped until Le Carré's fiction). And in recent years the hero's own agency—whether the CIA, MI6, or some unnamed and unidentified apparatus—poses a threat to him, as in *Three Days of the Condor, The Honourable Schoolboy,* the *Berlin Game/Mexico Set/London Match* trilogy, or in the recent films *Enigma* and *The Whistle Blower.*

Because the genre is so young, its major thematic signposts stand out clearly, and we can see the roles and positions of important contributers to this tradition. The first modern spy novel—as opposed to the first contemporary one—is James Fenimore Cooper's *The Spy* (1821). Surprisingly, he understood the natural habitat of the spy in the world as well as in fiction. With great imaginative interpolation he saw what it would be like to live a life in shadow, detached from society—to live in friendless solitude, a confidante of no one. Even more impressively, Cooper's perceptions are still true of the spy, real and fictional, today. Isolation, secrecy, estrangement, intrigue, betrayal, deceit, hypocrisy, darkness and shadow, paranoia—the spy's world is without trust or certitude, a world in which he can rely on no one, in which everyone is actively or potentially his enemy. After Cooper, until nearly the end of the century, aside from some dime novelists and a few other popular tale spinners, narrative writers did not bother with the possibilities of the genre. Cooper's insights were for the most part lost. The times were not right for fictions about espionage: spies were disreputable, not a proper subject for fiction in the nineteenth century.

Spying had never been an occupation of honor. Public morality held that it was not a task appropriate for gentlemen. Except for a brief flurry of interest during and shortly after the Civil War, spies and spying did not attract the public's attention for the rest of the century; the subject and its attendant themes were left almost entirely to a few American popular novelists and the writers of pulp thrillers in Great Britain. Early in the twentieth century, owing in part to the Dreyfus affair, there was a renewed interest in espionage. Cooper's pioneering perceptions had to be reinvented in order for later writers to express what he had seen nearly a century before.

Near the end of the nineteenth century, the political situation in Europe was viewed with suspicion and apprehension by a number of British writers. They expressed their fears in fictions depicting the great war they imagined was soon to come, a genre that has since been named the "imaginary war novels". Few of these fictions are read or even remembered today. How many recall George Chesney's "The Battle of Dorking," or William LeQueux's *Spies of the Kaiser,* or even Conan Doyle's "The Bruce-Partington Plans"? In these narratives, most of which were written during the last decades of the nineteenth century and the first years of this one, the occupation of the spy—traditionally suspect and even further in disrepute (thanks in large measure to the Dreyfus affair)—became a metaphor for the suspicion then felt by many Englishmen about other Europeans: the French, the Russians, and especially the Germans. In the imaginary war novels, England was pitted against one or another of these potential enemies. There was always something deceitful and treacherous about the foreign agents in these books; they never fought like gentlemen, out in the open, in the open air. They were not honorable; in a word they did not fight fair.

The plots of many post-Cooper popular spy novels focused on the schemes of foreign undercover agents or of patriotic English civilians who gathered intelligence from potential, or actual, enemies. Almost by accident, however, good spy novels were occasionally written. In 1903 Erskine Childers, somewhat under the influence of the pulp thrillers of the times, produced *The Riddle of the Sands,* which relates the seaborne adventures of two English yachtmen, ostensibly on holiday, and their surreptitious investigation of German war preparations in the Frisian Islands. So powerful and convincing was this book that Winston Churchill said that one result was to station the English battle fleet at Invergordon, Firth of Forth, and Scapa Flow.

Both of Childers's sailors are gentlemen amateurs acting out of an altruistic patriotism. Davies, the boat's owner, stumbles (or, more accurately, drifts) across what he feels are suspicious circumstances and characters off the north coast of Germany. He urges his friend, Caruthers, who works for the Foreign Office, to join him, and only when they are at sea does he reveal his suspicions. Distrusting the Foreign Office's bureaucracy, both men decide to investigate the situation and the shady characters themselves. Because they are gentlemen, they never dirty their hands in the messier aspects of espionage: fighting, lying, killing. They do not have to fight, they do not have to become involved in elaborate deceptions other than to conceal from their German acquaintances the fact that they are suspicious of aggressive German military and naval aims among the Frisian sands. And they certainly never have to take a life. They display only a gentleman's kind of deception, and whatever lies they have to tell are forgiven them because they must tell them for their country. Women are treated with distant Edwardian respect; Davies may be enamored of the daughter of one of the suspicious Germans, but their relationship is so hermetic that it can be hardly said to be sexual.

Sexuality as such is not even an issue in Joseph Conrad's *The Secret Agent* (1907), still one of the best books in English to deal with the clandestine life. It relates with poignant irony the activities of a secret agent, in place in London, in the employ of an unnamed Slavic embassy. As usual, Conrad is more interested in character than in narrative formulas; in *The Secret Agent* his targets are a group of international anarchists, necessarily clandestine, one of whom is incidentally a spy—a "secret agent." He is a comfortably married anarchist, the bourgeois owner of a small shop in London. For eleven years, the embassy's man complains, he has done nothing to justify his pay as an agent provocateur. And though ostensibly a secret agent, he is known by the police as well as his friends as a radical with radical connections, mild and sedentary as he is. This novel is said to have been inspired by an actual anarchist attempt to blow up the Greenwich observatory; and though Conrad's agent is goaded into attempting such demented wantonness, he is essentially docile and domesticated, with few of the concerns of those who inhabit the world of shadows.

Conrad always sought to infuse his fiction with psychological profundity—interesting and intelligent characters aesthetically depicted. In this concern, one of his contemporary foils was John Buchan, whose enormously influential *The Thirty-Nine Steps* (1915) placed the amateur spy more on a wartime footing: the professional agents are German, and Buchan's South African adventurer, Richard Hannay, also an amateur gentleman (of sorts) sets himself the task of bringing them to justice. Hannay is another in the then-lengthening line of gentleman agents, another counterspy who runs to ground the fiendish, foreign enemies of the empire.

Giving their fictional spies an amateur (and often gentlemanly) status enabled spy novelists to make them noble enough to be fictional heroes. Napoleon once commented that the only fitting reward for a spy was gold. Since spies were held to be morally degenerate and socially deficient, the first spy novelists found that it was necessary to make their fictional agents altruistic and patriotic gentlemen, which virtues made their activities acceptable. Davies and Caruthers "spied" only on behalf of and in defense of England. Hannay was not a spy himself, but an ad hoc counterspy, bringing to justice the malign agents of an evil foreign power. He could remain morally impeccable since his defensive deeds revealed the treachery of the German conspiracy. Hannay, along with Caruthers before him, and many after, were clubmen, with all the mannered affectations and social standing that such membership entailed (Usborne, 1953). What could be more British?

What were some of the thematic possibilities of the spy novel? It describes a quality of life, the individual's role within an impersonal and potentially hostile society, and his/her stance toward others. The topography in which the main characters operate is shadowy and full of concealed dangers. In Cooper, this terrain is the no-man's land between the combatants during the American Revolution, what he called "the Neutral ground." In Childers, it is the islet and sand-bar region off the Frisian coast, where the two Englishmen are alone, isolated, forced back upon their own resources. What more striking metaphor for the solitariness of the spy than two men in a small boat on the open sea? Conrad's secret agent has settled down comfortably and lives a sedate middle-class life in London—but it is a London that is politically docile. Buchan's Hannay, at first mistakenly thought to be a murderer, is from nearly the beginning on the run from the English police, then from the German agents.

Danger is everywhere. The spy must be mobile, and his intentions invisible if he is to survive. Buchan's locale is England but Hannay is usually in disguise, having to conceal his identity at first in order to escape confinement and later in order to misdirect his prey. It is a subterranean England that few Englishmen ever experience. The spy novel's characters, their motives and intentions, their loyalties and their functions, are seldom apparent. In Cooper's novel several characters appear in disguise, including George Washington at the story's end, so that for most of the narrative the reader is not quite sure who "the spy" of the title is. Conrad's secret agent runs a book store, but that is only his cover. Childers's investigators of the "riddle" are vacationing civilian Englishmen, but they must pretend to the Germans they meet that they are naive sailors who see nothing unusual in their days at sea. Hannay, on the run from the police, runs into the country house of a bald archaeologist, where he at first assumes that he is safe but shortly discovers that his host is the chief agent for the "other" side. Instead of achieving safety he has run into the vipers' nest.

Some of the political and philosophical questions implied by the existence of the spy in a modern democracy of course never occurred to

Cooper—or to Childers, or Buchan, or even Conrad. We cannot be too critical of these writers. When they wrote the idea of clandestinity was not in itself held to be ominous—was, as we might expect, not thought about much at all. Secret bureaucracies with the size and power of today's espionage agencies were undreamed of. To Childers, Buchan, or Conrad (or Cooper for that matter) spying was a private issue primarily concerning one's concept of one's own morals, not a world event that involves the individual and his sense of conscience regarding a complex of social and political issues. Spying was not widely practiced. The idea could not have occurred to any of these writers of a clandestine agency with the power to alter the course of the world and of millions of lives. The world was simpler then. Only governments with evil intent employed agents to perform their deceitful duties.

In this shadow world of even the early espionage fiction, danger—whether in the form of unmasking, imprisonment, capture, or physical harm—lurks everywhere. No one is to be trusted. Anyone, at any moment, may turn against you. The spy's precarious existence depends upon his invisibility and on his freedom of movement. If he is discovered, if he is restricted in his movement, he is finished. Of necessity he lives a double life—one of the surface (his cover), and one in which he acts out his true intentions. Cooper's Harvey Birch wears the disguise of an itinerant peddler—his cover is that of a secondhand goods salesman—his real occupation is as a spy for Washington. To persevere, to function effectively as the latter, he must continually maintain the guise of the former. Buchan's Richard Hannay—the exemplar of the heroic mode—is clever and resourceful, not merely cunning and certainly not at all deceitful. He himself admits that he always had a knack for figuring out codes and puzzles, and once he can stop running from his own police he quickly figures out the meaning—and the location—of the thirty-nine steps. Earlier, when the enemy spies lock him in a barn, he moves quickly to some dynamite lying conveniently in a corner, and blasts his way to freedom. On the run, he proves himself the master of several different disguises.

Secrecy, duplicity, treachery, concealed dangers, shadows, and night—the mainstream spy novel in this century embodies these images, episodes, and themes. Hannay's two-fisted adventures stand somewhat apart from this world. Near the end of *The Thirty-Nine Steps,* when he has identified himself to the police (who admit, in their turn, that they had for a long time known of his innocence), he is encouraged to take charge of the counterattack on the enemy's "Black Stone" conspirators. This almost miraculous assumption of authority comes about because the officers of the British Intelligence apparatus recognize in him a superior being who knows the details of the conspiracy better than they, a natural gentleman who exudes leadership at every pore. The admirals are only too happy to turn the direction of this counterespionage operation over to this civilian amateur South African who has appeared suddenly in their midst, who has all the answers, who can size up a man's character infallibly at a glance.

After Buchan, in the era of the sinister mode espionage novel, the spy is considerably humanized, that is, he is given quite human character flaws and several failings in basic tradecraft skills. Eric Ambler, writing in the later 1930s, is fond of placing his amateur in the midst of a plot he cannot handle by himself. Ambler's spy is usually a neophyte over his head in the hard-ball world of international espionage.

Graham Greene's heroes run a parallel course. "D," the confidential agent in the book of that name, is in civilian life a university lecturer, an expert on the *Song of Roland* as it happens. On his way to London he is mistrusted by those he meets, gets beaten up, and arrives late—with two teeth knocked out. No one trusts him. He in turn wisely suspects everyone he encounters. When his identity papers are stolen, he cannot prove who he is to the British coal executives from whom he wishes to buy—his confidential mission. In the end his mission fails (though that of the agent of the "other side" does also), and he is lucky to make his escape back to his homeland, where the worst thing people have to look forward to is dying.

Fleming sidestepped contemporary trends in espionage fiction. He said that he wanted to write spy novels, and we have always thought of him as a spy novelist, but in fact he wrote adventure stories. Few of Bond's adversaries are professional KGB agents, for instance. They often have, like Blofeld, Drax, or Goldfinger, schemes of more cosmic scope on their minds; usually they want to blackmail England or irradiate the gold in Fort Knox rather than engage in the usual activities of espionage agents. James Bond is solidly in the heroic mode of adventure novel heroes, while most of Fleming's spy novelist contemporaries have, following Le Carré, created heroes in the ironic mode.

In Sapper's *Bulldog Drummond. His Four Rounds With Carl Peterson,* one of the enemy is Steinemann, "of the common order of German. . . . He ate and drank enormously, and evidently considered that nothing further was required of him" (Sapper, p. 7). When Drummond was captured and taunted he was enraged; as Sapper tells us later when he has escaped, "to be laughed at by some dirty swine whom he could strangle in half a minute—was impossible!" (p. 85). Killing them was less involving than dispatching vermin. In fact, it was for Drummond somewhat satisfying. In killing the German enemy, he declares, "I'm sorry about it; I wasn't particularly anxious to end your life. But it had to be done." And thus was the Boche dead (p. 208). Germans were not the only ones qualmlessly killed; witness Bulldog's vituperations against a Russian victim: "I don't know which distresses me most, your maggoty brain or your insanitary appearance" (p. 140). Another memorable feature of Drummond was his fastidious tastes. Like Bond after him, Drummond smokes individually rolled cigarettes, in his case made of half Turkish and half Virginian tobacco. Like most English gentlemen, Drummond was anti-Semitic: in *Black Gang,* Drummond tells two Jews that "my friends do not like your trade, you swine," and then beats them up (McCormick, p. 194).

The character of Bond looks back, then, to the heroic-mode heroes Hannay and Drummond, to their chauvinism, their racism, their physicality, their sense of adventure. In these ways, the character of James Bond is an anachronism. Bond is not at home in darkness and shadow, and seldom visits this kind of world. He rarely solves the crime, or captures the villain, or accomplishes his mission through intellection. James Bond the professional secret agent, the hard-as-nails seducer of many women, the two-fisted tough guy, is unlike the "old time" spies of literature—agents who were out in the cold around the turn of the century—gentlemen patriots like Childers's Caruthers, or Maugham's Ashenden. Kingsley Amis has pointed out that Bond is a spy only in *From Russia, with Love;* in other novels he is not, though he often acts as a counterspy (1965, p. 1). Bond is identified as a member of the Secret Service in *The Spy Who Loved Me,* but only after he has driven off into the sunset. Unlike any real undercover agent, he always introduces himself by his correct name: "Bond, James Bond." In the best adventurer and hardboiled detective (rather than spy) tradition, he is handy with his fists, quick with his gun, does not hesitate to kill when he judges the situation right, and has an almost superhuman ability to withstand torture—the most diabolic torture that a sadistic enemy could inflict on him (in *Dr. No, Goldfinger,* and *Casino Royale*).

According to Amis, sexual interpretations of Bond's sufferings are mistaken; the torture scenes are episodes of realism, not subliminal sexuality. For contrast he cites Bulldog Drummond who also was frequently caught and eventually escaped but who was rarely tortured (1965, p. 13). Bond's adventures are more realistic, the hero more human—if we consider suffering torture to be symptomatic of the human condition. Yet because of Fleming's sensitivity to criticism—both he and Ann railed at the "sex, snobbery, and sadism" charge—*Goldfinger* was the last book in which Bond was captured and tortured.

Like the heroic era secret agents of old, Bond is an adventurer, and like them he is a heroic figure accustomed to winning. We cannot imagine James Bond as a nameless cog in a bureaucracy, as helpless as most of Eric Ambler's central characters, as humanly weak or as victimized as Graham Greene's "D." And we cannot imagine Bond enmeshed in one of the intricate webs that Len Deighton weaves around his characters. Ann Boyd asserts that for Le Carré, Deighton, and Adam Hall, the secret agent is "a dirty pawn on the chessboard of international politics" and espionage in fiction is just another dirty "organization game" (p. 58); we could never think of Bond as a pawn—dirty or clean. But neither can we imagine Bond exercising his intellect as does Le Carré's Smiley, a supreme detective and counterspy, a master of the contest of espionage-as-chess game. James Bond swims or skis his way into the enemy's stronghold, and then shoots or beats or murders his way out.

Like the earlier heroic-mode adventure novel heroes, James Bond does not live in a world of shadows. Bond is identified as a secret agent, we are told that he works for the Secret Service, but he does little of the work that secret agents in contemporary spy novels do. He is not continually plotted against (as is Deighton's Bernie Samson in the *Berlin Game*/*Mexico Set*/*London Match* trilogy); nor is he betrayed as are many of Le Carré's central figures. No enemy agents lurk in dimly lit doorways in Fleming's narratives. If Le Carré is correct that the modern spy novelist is only as good as his paranoia, Fleming is only marginally a spy novelist.

Fleming's remark that his contemporaries lacked genuine heroes is germane. He had read Sapper and John Buchan, and was greatly influenced by them. Those worthies of Fleming's adolescence, particularly Hannay, conquered German enemies; the world menace in our time is Russian, whether in the form of the KGB, or SMERSH, or their evil successor in Fleming's fiction, SPECTRE. Bond subdues their agents and foils their plots not with cunning but with strength and endurance. And with one of his trusty guns—as in *Live and Let Die, Diamonds Are Forever, From Russia, with Love, Doctor No,* or *The Spy Who Loved Me.*

Drummond or Hannay might have found it necessary to inflict bodily harm from time to time. Neither one, Drummond especially, ever flinched from it. But neither Sapper nor Buchan ever gave their heroes a "license to kill," which is the significance of Bond's "007" designation. Fleming appeals to the id directly. One of the attractions of the fictional spy is his ability to violate the laws of our society with impunity. And while we all acknowledge the civil and moral restraints against taking human life, there is a fascination in vicariously being able to do so. On some unconscious level we want to kill our enemies, but since we cannot in reality relieve ourselves of these feelings, James Bond can do it for us. He is allowed to kill not, we are led to understand, on his personal behalf, but for God, country, and the Service. (Only once—in *For Your Eyes Only*—does he plan to murder for more personal reasons, and then it is to revenge a wrong done the friends of his chief, "M.") If Bond does not kill his (and our) enemies, he can beat them with his fists. Unlike Greene's "D," Bond would never be pushed around the countryside, would never be intimidated by thugs or beaten up on the roadside, would never lose teeth to another's fists. When Bond escapes, as from Blofeld's mountain sanitorium in the Swiss Alps, it is not the flight of a frightened and defeated man.

For several reasons, Bond is hard to take seriously. Because Fleming was not interested in life in the shadows, in the life of the spy as it is really lived today, but instead wanted to write heroic adventures, realism went out the window. Unlike the world of other contemporary spies, the world of James Bond is nearly entirely fantastic. Although other secret agents of our acquaintance—Samson, Smiley, Quiller, Leamas, Scylla—are fictional, their lives are set ostensibly in the real world, a world we know something about, where the CIA and MI6 are in the trenches against the KGB and its Warsaw Pact subordinates. Their experiences could have happened: their authors make us believe in them to that extent. But Fleming forgoes that verisimilitude. We can hardly believe in the reality of Dr. No, Hugo Drax, Mr. Big, Goldfinger, Blofeld. We cannot believe that the world is in danger from the likes of such mythical organizations as SMERSH or SPECTRE. While Fleming has had some success in drawing readers into this far-side-of-the-moon passed off as reality, this is fantasyland stuff.

Not all implausible plots are handled so fantastically. Len Deighton's *Spy Story*, for instance, involves an alleged plot to steal an atomic bomb. Unlikely as that scenario is (the "theft" is only pretended, and is not even attempted by the self-proclaimed "thief"), Deighton carries it off by careful craftsmanship, creating a number of believable characters. We are led to think that it might be real—that such a situation could happen. Not so in *Thunderball,* with its highjacking of a British bomber, crashlanded under water where it is stored; its cast of unlikely characters; its blackmailing of Western governments; its glitzy underwater combat film sequence to decide the issue. In *On Her Majesty's Secret Service* (1963), Blofeld plans to infect Britain with crop and livestock pests. This most elaborate scheme is to be realized with the unwitting help of several young ladies (each quite sensual and beautiful, fortunately for James Bond) who, when discharged from Blofeld's mountain rest home will carry deadly toxins back to Britain with them when they return. When John Gardner made a similar plot the basis of *The Dancing Dodo* (1978), which is unbelievable in its own way—an old Nazi plan to loose plague bacteria in England is revived when neo-Nazis find the lethal cylinders and plant them in present-day London—the details of the scenario are somehow more plausible. Gardner is able to make us believe in the situation. We feel the characters' tension as they move through the events of the novel. We see a villain much more human than those Fleming was able to create. The minor characters seem like people we might one day meet, and there is no clutch of nubile, mindless young women to tax our credulity.

Ian Fleming had great appeal for Englishmen of the 1950s and 1960s; he gave them an upbeat message at a time when his contemporaries pictured the world as a place full of treachery, deceit, and dark shadows where hidden dangers from unknown sources are constant threats. The further reaches of Bond's world—the British Empire, the power of Great Britain—may be somewhat ragged on the fringes. For some it seems more important than ever to cling to the beliefs of the old Empire. During the first few decades of this century the racism and the smug imperialism of Hannay and Drummond were not as offensive as they are to us today. Bond, because of Fleming's biases, shares these attitudes toward the "inferior races," but the worldwide might of England is a wistful memory. A certain defensive quality tints all of Bond's attitudes toward his country. He is as patriotic as anyone, unquestionably, but the object of that patriotic faith must not strike English readers as being as solid or as indestructable as it once had been.

Because Bond did little bona fide spying—he was not a secret agent in the manner of such real spies as Fuchs, Burgess, MacLean, and

Philby—Fleming never exploited the potential of the genre. The themes, ideas, concerns packed into the novels of Le Carré, or Deighton, or fifty other contemporary writers for that matter—ideas that Greene and Ambler exploited in the late thirties—pass by Fleming in the night. Questions of loyalty and betrayal, trust and suspicion, faith and doubt, hypocrisy and obligation, the moral ontology of a clandestine agency within an ostensibly open and free society—all of these issues are unavailable to the readers of Fleming because they were never dreamed of in the philosophy of Fleming himself.

In this deeper sense Fleming was not a spy novelist. He did not know what the spy novel was about, what its possibilities were. He called his adventurer a "spy," and placed him within a bureaucracy that he labeled an espionage apparatus. But the association of James Bond with spying was only skin-deep; it did not go down to the bone.

In the 1950s the reading public in England and the United States was weary of the devastating war recently ended and fearful of an atomic holocaust to come. The Korean War dragged on, the Empire was crumbling away, England had failed to capture the Suez Canal, several of its diplomats were exposed as Russian agents. People grew wary of unqualified patriotism. And the facile clichés about good and evil, their side and ours, right and wrong, justice and corruption lost their appeal, too many people having died in two great wars, each of which was fought to end all wars. And despite the actual battlefield heroics of the preceding decade, even the centuries-old virtue of heroism had become suspect. In the fiction of the time, the antihero emerged. In the fiction of espionage the spy was humanized, and shown to be as riddled with flaws and insecurities as the rest of us. In this historical/cultural milieu Ian Fleming began publishing the James Bond novels, adventure stories that were new only in that they were updates of the kind of adventure spy stories that had been popular three and four decades earlier. More often than not, spies in contemporary fiction are victimized—by the enemy, by their own agencies, by the ruthlessly determined—but Fleming set out to write books in which the hero could persevere and triumph. Much is explained by his remark that "I think the reason for his [Bond's] success is that people are lacking heroes in real life today" (*New Yorker,* 1962, 32–34).

Thus—though the character of Bond was not carefully drawn, nor his adventures intricately or tightly plotted—he soon enjoyed a phenomenal success. Only one of Fleming's Bond novels sold fewer than two million copies, and that was his last one, written hurriedly before his death. Bond's fame is probably greater than that of any fictional character of this century, surpassing Scarlett O'Hara and Mike Hammer, rivalling Sherlock Holmes and Bulldog Drummond.

Bond's popularity wasn't all trivial; serious people read about, or at least had heard about him. Chapman Pincher, a British journalist who is an expert in Intelligence matters, took a moment out in his book *Too Secret Too Long* to guess that naturalist and broadcaster Maxwell Knight—who referred to himself as "M"—may have been Fleming's source for this character (no one else thinks so). In *Ways of Escape,* Graham Greene reflected that his ambition after the war was "to write a novel of espionage free from the conventional violence, which has not, in spite of James Bond, been a feature of the British Secret Service" (p. 227). In Greene's *The Human Factor,* two British Intelligence evaluators, Castle and Davis, are chatting about personal matters. Davis daydreams about a posh assignment in Africa and the life he might realize there with his lovely secretary. Castle exclaims that he thought Davis preferred a bachelor's life; Davis answers, "I wasn't talking about marriage. Bond never had to marry" (p. 49). Why shouldn't he be like Bond? He, Davis, is a real spy. Later, talking to his stepson, Castle reflects that there are still fathers around who tell their children about the existence of God: Sam responds, "Spies like 007?" (p. 59). Not exactly, but Bond is continually on the youngster's mind. On a family picnic, his conversation turns again to that most famous of spies: Davis provokes Sam by saying that his fountain pen is really a gas gun whose knob squirts "nerve gas," and that James Bond was never allowed one like it—"it's too secret" (p. 98). Later still, chief of security Daintry encounters someone who calls him "one of the hush-hush boys. James Bond and all that" (p. 184).

In Len Deighton's thriller—which treats, in part, the difference between professionals and amateurs, field men and desk men—Etonian amateur Henry Tiptree wants to be thrilled by stories of espionage and adventure: he wants Samson, a professional, to tell him "that there is at least one James Bond johnny out there risking his neck among the Russkies" (p. 217). The allusion to Bond shows that Tiptree, like Castle's young son, operates largely in a fantasy world. Earlier, Tiptree exclaims that "you London Central people really do see life. . . . Have you really been doing a James Bond caper, Dicky? Have you been crossing swords with the local Russkies?" (p. 117).

When William Goldman's Marathon Man first meets his dissertation director, Professor Biesenthal quotes a line from *Goldfinger*: "the first time it's coincidence, the second time it's happenstance, the third time it's enemy action" (Goldman, 1974, p. 46). Bryan Forbes's recent book *The Endless Game* (1987) has an English agent tell a politician acquaintance about a BBC journalist assassinated several years earlier with a poison-tipped umbrella; the other replies that it is "very James Bond stuff" and further that Ian Fleming "had too vivid an imagination. Reduced the whole thing to a kid's game. Bad thing, imagination" (pp. 50–51). David Cornwell (John Le Carré) described his most famous Intelligence operative, George Smiley—a cult figure in his own right—as different "in every way that I can think off" from James Bond, but still, "ultimately, the reluctant servant of established Western society." William Stevenson, a friend, remarked that "it was straight out of James Bond"—referring not to any violence (there was none), but to the tight-lipped self control and simplicity of the service (Stevenson, 1983, p. 18).

And, of all people, the infamous Kim Philby, remembering the attempts to unravel a particularly knotty World War II problem encountered during his tenure in British Intelligence, "doubted whether anyone on our side would really welcome a James Bond–like free-for-all." Philby's associate, former assistant director of MI 5, Peter Wright, expressed doubt about the genuineness of self-confessed defector Oleg Penkovsky, with the remark that it seemed to him "to smack more of James Bond than of real life" (*Spycatcher*, p. 209). Phillip Knightley's *The Second Oldest Profession* (1986) meditates on international espionage agencies and their proliferation since 1945: "No, it is not all over for James Bond yet. Bond and his employers in Washington, London, Moscow, or wherever are thriving in the 1980s" (p. 381).

Writers like Wright and Knightley feel free to let Bond's name stand for everyone who shares his occupation. A James Bond is any spy, anywhere. The chapter in which Knightley's reference occurs details the great multiplication of espionage and covert activities in spy agencies today, and talks about activities undreamed of in Fleming's imagination. Despite the development of all of the electronic snoopers, the technocrats, the spy satellite evaluators, the crateologists, Bond has become the symbol—instantly apprehended throughout the world—of a spy. He never did many of the things that real spies may do today, yet his aura spreads over all of them, over all of their business. If they are "spies," they are James Bonds.

Much less famous, at least in the West, is the adventure of Leakh

Narayan Bhoge, a Guyanese graduate student enrolled in New York's Queens College. Approached by KGB agent Gennadi Zakharov, Leakh decided almost at once to become a double agent, reporting all of the Russian's moves to the FBI. When the Russian had been arrested and charged with espionage, and Leakh's ordeal was over (he was not a professional agent), he was reported to be waiting for "the sports cars and beautiful girls of the James Bond movies he had always enjoyed" (*New York*, 6 April 1987, p. 38). Spy movies were among Leakh's adolescent passions, and Sean Connery was his favorite actor (p. 39).

The French structuralist critic Roland Barthes used a passage from *Goldfinger* to illustrate sequential logic in narrative: "When we are told that—the telephone ringing during night duty at Secret Service headquarters—*Bond picked up one of the four receivers,* the moneme *four* in itself constitutes a functional unit, referring as it does to a concept necessary to the story (that of a highly developed bureaucratic technology)" (Reader, p. 263). Barthes may not be entirely ingenuous here; he may be quoting Fleming just to annoy his academic readers. No admiration may be intended—Genette based his critical system on Proust, Aristotle on Homer—yet, for whatever reason, Fleming is quoted and Bond appears in serious critical writing (however ironically intended), which further bespeaks his fame in all spheres of modern society.

Richard M. Bissell, former deputy director and chief of clandestine services of the CIA during the Eisenhower and early Kennedy years, told *Los Angeles Times* reporter Leonard Klady ("Calendar", 26 July 1987, p. 3) that "one could argue Kennedy wanted to adopt the style of the [Fleming] novels into the working operations of the agency. That seems quite apparent when you examine operations after the Bay of Pigs."

Perhaps the most touching and probably the most telling tribute to the international reputation of James Bond was the naming of an island for him in southwest Thailand. In Phang Nga Bay is "James Bond Island." *The Man with the Golden Gun* and *Goldfinger* have been filmed, in part, in this extraordinarily beautiful part of the world, on Koh Khao Ping island. The bay has numerous rock islands. It is near Phuket, less than an hour's flight from Bangkok. This must be the only real estate—at least in the Orient—named for a fictional character.

Despite the claims of theologians such as Ann Boyd—who feels that beneath Fleming's snide and sophisticated surface was a deep and abiding concern for the great sin of our day, sloth or accidie—Fleming strikes nearly all readers as barely interested in the condition of his world. The decline of a once powerful and influential empire is a serious matter. It is part of the challenge of what might have been confronted by Fleming's fiction, but he preferred to write narratives that blended farce and melodrama, fictions that laboriously wove lists of fact into situations and plots that were ridiculous (Van Dover, p. 182). The resulting generic and thematic blend has, nevertheless, produced a character who remains in our collective consciousness. Despite the flawed fictions in which he appears, the "cardboard booby" has taken on a life of his own. It is re-created continually in our own imaginations (demonstrating that there is something of James Bond in many of us), living somehow despite Fleming's creative shortcomings, yet another persuasive argument for the reader's active role in character creation. Hamlet, Lear, and Falstaff demand no such effort. The genius can be said to be within the text, and the reader's participation need never be called into accountability. But when a storyteller presents us with dull characters being shunted through implausible plots, and one of those characters remains lastingly in our memories, the receptor's creativity must be involved. Much, but not all, of the help the reader has received comes from Broccoli and Saltzman, producers of the Bond films, and from Sean Connery, their first star. Nevertheless, Fleming must be given credit for having roused in so many millions such willingness to become co-creators of their own illusion.

Chapter Seven
Bond, Women, and Wogs

Fleming has been most frequently criticized for his treatment of women and ethnic minorities. We are now a great deal more sensitive toward these subjects than when Fleming wrote, and certainly more than when he was growing up and interiorizing the attitudes manifested in his fiction. Nigel West has suggested to us that Fleming's racism expressed the prevailing biases of "polite society"—that his bigotry was no more intense than that of many of the "right" people. But many American readers, coming to Fleming for the first time, are angered by what they read in his pages regarding ethnic minorities and women. We can find something in his writing offensive to nearly everyone. Where to begin? Since his attitude toward races other than the Anglo-Saxon is less blatant than his derogation of women, we will start with that.

Umberto Eco has pointed out that Fleming's villains are, to Englishmen, racial "others." It is as Vivien Michel's boyfriend says when explaining why they must break off their relationship: his parents have "ridiculous ideas about 'foreigners,'" although he protests that he regards her like any "any other English girl." And he adores her accent—she is Canadian (*The Spy Who Loved Me,* p. 42). Eco does not discuss the influence of Buchan and Sapper on Fleming, and so does not mention that all of Bond's opponents are from the same ethnic molds as are Hannay's and Drummond's. Mr. Big is a Haitian black with a face like that of a waterlogged corpse. American Jack Spang is a red-haired humpback whose eyes might have been rented from a taxidermist. Hugo Drax's face is badly disfigured from botched plastic surgery; apparently born in Liverpool, he is in fact German; and, most unclublike, he cheats at cards. Dr. No is of mixed German and Chinese origin. Goldfinger's ethnic origin is Baltic, though he is suspected of having Jewish blood (his obsession with gold is a telling point). Blofeld has a Polish father and a Greek mother. Le Chiffre is from mixed Mediterranean and Prussian/Polish blood; his small ears with large lobes disclose his Jewish heritage. In short, Fleming's villains are, as Kingsley Amis listed them, Bulgars, Corsicans, Germans, Italians, Yugoslavs, Koreans, Russians, Sicilians, Turks, Spanish-Americans, Chigroes, and Americans (p. 75). Though for Amis this is just a bit of Fleming's healthy patriotism showing through.

In *Casino Royale* Bond's friend Mathis tells him that there are two Bulgarians in the town. "They are stupid, but obedient," we learn, "the Russians use them for simple killings or as fall-guys for more complicated ones" (p. 27). Mostly they are used against Turks or Yugoslavs; in *Casino Royale* they are used against Bond, and they fail. The French are not quite so contemptible, but they "all" suffer from liver complaints (p. 30). No ethnic group (other than the English) is really safe from insult; at one point in *Goldfinger* Bond drinks some Enzian, "the firewater distilled from gentian that is responsible for Switzerland's chronic alcoholism" (p. 157). At the gaming table he sizes up the opposition; a Greek who owns, as all Eastern Mediterranean people do, a profitable shipping line (p. 66); a small-time maharajah with all his wartime sterling balances to play with. Bond knows, we are told, that few of the Asiatic races are courageous gamblers, and that even the Chinese lose heart "if the going was bad" (p. 67). Many would not think being a bad gambler such a bad thing; in the world of James Bond it is a major character failing. There is also an Italian, "who possibly had plenty of money from rack-rents in Milan" and could be expected to play a dashing and foolish game, though he might also "lose his temper and make a scene" (p. 67).

In *Live and Let Die* Bond gets his assignment from "M" during whose interview he ruminates about the possible opposition: "I don't think I've ever heard of a great Negro criminal before . . . Chinamen, of course, the men behind the opium trade. They've been some big-time Japs, mostly in pearls and drugs. Plenty of Negroes mixed up in diamonds and gold in Africa . . ." (pp. 16–17). But Negroes have some talents, after all. "They've got plenty of brains and ability and guts," Bond laments, but now Moscow has taught one of them "the technique" (p. 17). A little later, in Harlem, Bond tells his American friend Leiter that, while the English are a bit superstitious (especially the Celts), that is nothing compared to the Negroes: "here one can almost hear the drums." In a nightclub shortly thereafter Bond could smell their "sweet, feral smell" (p. 47). They are "these people" (p. 94).

The Germans (in *Moonraker*) have "the usual German chips on their shoulder" (p. 80). When Bond calls Hugo Drax a "Kraut," he is incensed, and replies, "a Kraut. Yes, I am indeed a *Reichdeutscher* . . . and even England will soon agree that they have been licked by just one single German. And then perhaps they'll stop calling us Krauts— BY ORDER" (p. 192). One of the bad guys in *Diamonds Are Forever*— but he *is* a bad guy, after all—complains that in his organization the weak links are the natives: "and you know these black swine. They can't stand a real beating" (pp. 6–7). And American gangsters are "mostly a lot of Italian bums with monogrammed shirts who spend the day eating spaghetti and meatballs and squirting scent all over themselves" (p. 18).

In *From Russia, with Love* it is the turn of the Turks—"dark, ugly, neat little officials were the modern Turks" (p. 113). Bond's Turkish friend, Darko Kerim, had a warm, firm Western handshake, "not the banana skin handshake of the East that makes you want to wipe your fingers on your coat-tails" (p. 118). At a restaurant, Kerim argues with a waiter and then tells Bond: "that is the only way to treat these damned people. They love to be cursed and kicked. It is all they understand. It is in the blood. All this pretense of democracy is killing them. They want some sultans and wars and rape and fun" (p. 129). Later, Kerim must caution Bond about walking in Istanbul's streets, for "garbage is a polite word for what my charming people throw into their streets" (p. 163). Yet Fleming does not forget that the Russians are the villains of the story, and at one point Kerim explains to Bond that in killing, "the Russians have not much finesse. They like mass death" (p. 159). Bond agrees; "they simply don't understand the carrot. Only the stick has any effect. Basically they're masochists. . . . That's why they were so happy under Stalin" (p. 168).

Doctor No has a wide scope for its contempt—so many racial and ethnic groups come into play. Of the Jamaicans, Bond learns from "M" that "sex and machete fights are about all they understand" (p. 25). British diplomat Pleydell-Smith (whom Bond respects) tells the secret agent that "the Jamaican is a kindly lazy man with the virtues and vices of a child. He lives on a very rich island but he doesn't get rich from it. He doesn't know how to and he's too lazy" (p. 57). Dr. No's minions are half Negro and half Chinese—Chigroes. "They've got some of the intelligence of the Chinese and most of the vices of the black man. The police have a lot of trouble with them" (p. 58). About to make his escape from Dr. No's clutches, Bond realizes at one point that he may have to shoot one of his guards. He does not like killing in cold blood (throughout the novels he kills thirty-eight or thirty-nine—according to Amis), "but these men would be Chinese negro gangsters, the strong-arm guards who did the dirty work. They would certainly be murderers many times over" (p. 213).

Goldfinger has its share of racism, but one is surprised by the intensity of some of Fleming's expression. In Miami, Bond looks down on the gardeners, "raking the paths and picking up leaves with the lethargic slow motion of coloured help" (pp. 23–24). Col. Smithers of the Secret Service tells Bond that Goldfinger's Korean servants are never any threat to the man's schemes because "they don't know a word of any civilized language" (p. 63). Goldfinger apologizes to his then guest Bond about the Koreans, his servants: "these people get easily overexcited" (p. 113). To impress Bond, Goldfinger orders his servant, Oddjob, to smash an oak banister with his hand. The Korean obeys, then comes to attention awaiting further orders. Next he is ordered to smash a carved wooden mantelplace seven feet off the floor; and with a three-step run he leaps into the air and snaps the wood in half with a chop of his feet. Again he comes to attention and awaits further orders. Goldfinger remarks to Bond that Oddjob is truly a lethal weapon, a fact that he and we, the readers, will remember later in the story when Bond will have to fight him. Then, to reward his servant, Goldfinger tosses him a cat from under his arm: "I am tired of seeing this animal around. You may have it for dinner" (p. 124).—"he regards them [cats] as a great delicacy" (p. 128). Later, Bond will become aware of "the sickly zoo-smell of Oddjob" (p. 174). Later still, when he is in Goldfinger's employ, pretending to assist him in his scheme to capture Fort Knox, he is no less contemptuous of Oddjob, and no less cruel than is Goldfinger. When he is hungry he orders, "quick march! Chop-chop. . . . Come on! Jump to it! Don't stand there looking inscrutable. I'm hungry." Goldfinger had decided to let Bond live, for some reason unknown to James. But as long as he is alive, he lives on his own terms, and that means "putting Oddjob and any other Korean firmly in his place, which, in Bond's estimation, was rather lower than apes in the mammalian hierarchy" (p. 181). Oddjob was, in Bond's more laconic moments, "that Korean ape" (p. 189).

Life with such servants is a trial for Goldfinger. When the champagne is served, Bond is bidden to help himself, as "these people are as likely to pour it into your plate as your glass" (p. 125). Why does Goldfinger employ such servants? We wonder about this relationship because of his frequently expressed contempt for Koreans. To Bond's query the answer is patiently given. The usual bodyguards are retired policemen, slow of reflex, perhaps open to bribes, with a respect for human life, but "The Koreans have no such feelings. . . . They are the cruelest, most ruthless people in the world" (p. 128). Oddjob was, for his master, an ideal example—"simple, unrefined clay, capable of limited exploitation" (p. 182). For the Korean's entertainment Goldfinger brings in street women from London, and though they are not much to look at, as he says, all the Koreans ask is that they be white, for it is their pleasure "to submit the white race to the grossest indignities" (p. 128). Sometimes there are accidents, but they can be covered up with money.

Something about the mysterious East roused Fleming's dander. In *You Only Live Twice,* set mainly in Japan, the targets are the Japanese who, like the Koreans, are not the villains, so Fleming's scorn of them is gratuitous. Although they have pretended to adopt democratic ways for the benefit of their American conquerors, they are unreconstructed: "once a Jap, always a Jap" is the evaluation of Australian diplomat R. L. Henderson in his briefing for Bond. The Japanese are a separate human species; scratch a Russian and you will find a Tartar, but scratch a Japanese and you will find a samurai; yet the end product is not even the real thing, only what they think is the real thing. "Most of this *samurai* is a myth, like the Wild West stuff the Americans are brought up on, or your knights in shining armor in King Arthur's court" (p. 36). When Bond agrees that there's a certain "aboriginal common sense" in what his diplomat friend says, he is, in turn, lashed with "don't talk to me about the aborigines!" He is outraged, as he tells James, that in Australia there is a move afoot to give the vote to the aborigines. And he, Henderson, wants no more of that "liberal crap" (p. 36). Japan, Bond learns, is "a country with an unquenchable thirst for the bizarre, the cruel, the terrible" (p. 99). As Henderson has told him, the Japanese have an "automatic ant-like subservience to discipline and authority . . . that had resulted in one of the great crimes of the century" (p. 128). The feeling is widespread among Fleming's characters, the bad as well as the good.

Almost all races and nationalities get rough treatment in the Bond novels. Sometimes the opinions expressed are those of villains, sometimes of friends and allies of Bond, sometimes those of Bond's colleagues and superiors in the Secret Service. Often they are expressed by Bond himself. Usually the slurs are direct and coarse, like those against

Koreans. Sometimes they ridicule: the Greeks are all said to own shipping lines. Sometimes the offensive evaluations are only slightly derogatory: the French and their universal liver trouble, the Swiss and their "chronic alcoholism." But whether by gratuitous insult or unflattering stereotype, Fleming's books single out individuals because of their ethnic heritage, and describe ethnic groups and nationalities in mindless ways that do not consider individual merit but merely condemn. In the world of Fleming and Bond, only the English are commendable.

Did Fleming believe this stuff himself? And if it occurs in the pages of his books with such consistency, for whom did he think he was writing? Given the plethora of explicit racist statements, other passages, which might have been inoffensive in themselves, also stand out. In *Live and Let Die* Bond is at one point surrounded by several blacks who rolled their eyes, "their teeth showing in delighted, cruel grins" (p. 191). The German in *Moonraker*, on seeing the corpse of a colleague, raises his left arm and shouts "Heil" before killing himself. Bond asks whether that was all that he said. "That's all, sir" is the answer; "Don't seem to be able to forget the bloody word, do they?" Bond replies thoughtfully, "no entourage, all sport mustaches: "handlebar, walrus, Kaiser, Hitler" (p. 105). How is the reader to take such an inverted stereotype as Bond's thought that if you "scratch a German [you'll] find precision"? (p. 117). Of the Italian gangsters in *Diamonds Are Forever*, Bond admits that he "used to think your gangsters [he's talking to American Tiffany Case] were just a bunch of Italian greaseballs who filled themselves up with pizza pie and beer all week and on Saturday knocked off a garage or a drugstore so as to pay their way at the races." But now that he has experience, he is forced to admit that "they've certainly got plenty of violence on the payroll" (p. 174).

Of course, not all racial or ethnic others are evil and animalistic. Occasionally a non-Englishman is forgiven his non-Englishness. Drax's friend and metal broker, Meyer, strikes Bond as a "nice chap. Jew. Very fine player" (*Moonraker*, p. 23). Or Bond's Jamaican friend, Quarrel, seems nearly as decent as a white man: "There was the blood of Cromwellian soldiers and buccaneers in him and his face was strong and angular and his mouth was almost severe. His eyes were grey. It was only the spatulate nose and the pale palms of his hands that were negroid" (*Live and Let Die*, p. 159). Bond likes Quarrel; perhaps he recognizes his English blood, manifest in his grey eyes. Bond himself feels somewhat ill at ease among the English, for like Fleming he is himself Scottish-born: "Bond knew that there was something alien and un-English about himself. He knew that he was a difficult man to cover up. Particularly in England" (*Moonraker,* p. 32). Is England so racist a society? We think that such attitudes are more individual than national. Fleming abhorred what he was afraid would swallow him: being considered a foreigner. Despite his aloof poses—perhaps because of them—he wanted to be accepted by mainstream English society; they, especially Ann's friends, were the "right" people.

What defense do critics offer for Fleming's racism? Virtually all acknowledge its existence. Laura Lilli, in a review essay of Fleming's critics (in Eco, 1966, p. 165 ff.) observes that "from Amis to Piovene, from Aristarco to Morvan Lebesque, no critic denies Fleming's racialism." Alberto Moravia saw in *Goldfinger* a symbolic racial struggle:

The evil Goldfinger employs for his crimes and his manipulations technicians and assassins of the yellow race, or beautiful but inhuman women of pure Aryan descent; in a world dominated by Goldfinger, Indo-Aryan robots would dedicate themselves to crime with the help of inferior Mongolian or Negro race. But James Bond is no less racialist than Goldfinger; and his successful fight in the caves of Fort Knox against Oddjob symbolises the struggle of the white race against the yellow.

Movie director Terence Young found in Fleming a Fascist tendency. For this critic 007 is the symbol of the myth of violence as the solution of conflict. The cudgel, once the destroyer of evil, is in Fleming replaced by the laser, ICBMs, and atomic bombs (p. 167).

Fleming's defenders in the matter of racism (or racialism, to be British), are of two ideological kinds. Either they think that Fleming's racism is not to be taken seriously (because he is not intense about it or his readers do not care very much), or they find nothing wrong with such attitudes. Fleming's most articulate defender from charges of racism is Umberto Eco (1966, p.60): "Fleming is a racialist in the sense that any artist is one if, to represent the devil, he depicts him with oblique eyes; in the sense that a nurse is one who, wishing to frighten children with the bogey-man, suggests that he is black." Eco sees this trait as a comprehensive one in Fleming's psyche: "It is singular that Fleming should be anti-Communist with the same lack of discrimination as he is anti-Nazi and anti-German. It isn't that in the one case he is reactionary and in the other democratic. He is simply Manichean for operative reasons: he sees the world as made up of good and evil forces in conflict." Fleming personifies the world—at least the world of James Bond—as a universal struggle between these two forces. But, Eco concludes, this does not make him either a racist or a Fascist, but rather a cynic who creates tales with simplified oppositional forces "for general consumption." If Fleming is reactionary it is because he makes such extensive use of stock figures, seeing the world in black and white, failing to recognize nuances and distinctions, refusing to admit contradictions, "always dogmatic and intolerant—in short, reactionary" (p. 61). Piovene acknowledges its presence, but does not think that Fleming's readers take it very seriously: "the purveyors of popular amusement, however, are in the habit of inserting . . . a pinch of political mythology of their own. . . . I do not believe that the spectators of 007 greatly mind those commonplaces of political mythology, discredited from the first by an obvious and complete lack of moral intentions" (p. 166).

A second approach is that of Fleming's champion, Amis, who sees nothing wrong in racism: "to use foreigners as villains is a convention older than our literature. It's not in itself a symptom of intolerance about foreigners. Mr. Fleming does not once allow Bond to fall into the *undifferentiated* xenophobia that's all over Sapper. But there's no hint of anti-Semitism, and no feeling about colour more intense than that, for instance, Chinese Negroes make good sinister-villain material (They do, too)" (p. 166). Amis praises Fleming's prejudice because he has made it knowledgeable: not all Turks are no good, but only the Turks of the plains. The trouble with Paris is not that its population is French, but that it has "pawned its heart to the Russians, Roumanians, Bulgars and Germans." And all the French suffer from liver complaints. "Any fool can dislike Chinese or Japanese; the smart man's best-hated Asian is the Korean" (pp. 166–67).

Can Amis be serious? Surely he shows himself to be an ironist here—but what then is our opinion of Fleming. And, as Amis points out—in a direct, nonironic statement—"nobody English does anything evil" (p. 166). But is not this the racism of Sapper all over again, though somewhat molified for postwar tastes? Moravia (again) finds in Bond a type "imposed on the eroticism of the whole world by the Anglo-Saxon hegemony" that does not represent moral virtue but a vitality "of a biological, sexual, racial kind, a virtue that is power, vigour, youth . . ." (p. 167). The primary moral difference between Bond and Gold-

finger, Moravia complains, is that women love Bond; morality in
Fleming is a biological force. And that brings us to Fleming's treatment of women in the Bond novels.

Eco catalogs the plights of most of Bond's women (1966, p. 48 ff.).
Vesper Lynd, an unwilling agent of the Russians, is being blackmailed
by Le Chiffre. Solitaire is the slave of the Negro gangster boss, Mr.
Big. Tiffany Case is dominated by the Spangs. Naive and trusting
Tatiana is unreflectingly obedient to Rosa Klebb and the KGB in general. Jill and Tilly Masterson and Pussy Galore work for Goldfinger;
they dislike him in varying degrees, but the pay is good. Domino
Vitali is the pawn of Blofeld, through the agency of her lover, Largo.
Blofeld hypnotically controls the English beauties in his Piz Gloria;
his associate, Irma Bunt, runs their lives like a drill sergeant. Honeychile Rider's situation is more complex; she is held captive by Dr. No
who tries to have the island's crabs kill her, and when a young girl she
had been raped back on the mainland. Gala Brand is Drax's secretary
and girl Friday, and therefore subservient to him though not coerced
into obedience like the others. And Kissy Suzuki's domination by Blofeld is "purely allegorical, shared by the whole population of the place"
(p. 49).

The pattern is consistent enough for Eco to establish an algorithm
which describes all of them.

1. The girl is beautiful and good.
2. She has been rendered frigid by severe adolescent trials.
3. She is thus conditioned to serve the villain.
4. Bond introduces her to an appreciation of human nature.
5. Bond possesses and liberates her but (with one exception) does not establish
   any lasting relationship.

A fairy-tale quality informs this model; it is by no means a unique or
even a particularly individual vision of relations with women, seen
from a man's point of view. It is not, however, the scenario we would
expect to find in contemporary fiction.

Knowing something about Fleming's life, we can see much of the
author's fantasies here. This is the man who in his notebooks made the
following aphoristic observations: "The woman likes the door to be
forced"; "You think more of the kiss than of the mouth—you want the

thing and not the person"; "As long as a woman's flesh is clean and healthy what does it matter what shape she is?" (Pearson, pp. 84–85). Like the hero of "Snow White and the Seven Dwarfs," Prince Charming/Bond will rescue the girl/woman/heroine from a life of sexual deprivation and then liberate her to pursue her own inclinations. Life has deprived her of an appreciation of the possibilities of human love. Bond's sexual encounter will change her life, releasing her from the bonds of evil. Sex conquers all.

But the Bond who emerges in the details of the novels is less than Prince Charming:

With most women his manner was a mixture of taciturnity and passion. The lengthy approaches to a seduction bored him almost as much as the subsequent mess of disentanglement. He found something grisly in the inevitability of the pattern of each affair. The conventional parabola—sentiment, the touch of the hand, the kiss, the passionate kiss, the feel of the body, the climax in the bed, then more bed, then less bed, then the boredom, the tears, and the final bitterness—was to him shameful and hypocritical.

(*Casino Royale*, p. 148)

One can understand that the ninety-odd women whom Fleming said he had seduced would produce in him the guilty ennui ascribed, above, to Bond. Two years later, in *Moonraker*, Bond's responses to his life are little changed (p. 9):

It was only two or three times a year that an assignment came along requiring his particular abilities. For the rest of the year he had the duties of an easy-going senior civil servant—elastic office hours from around ten to six; lunch, generally, in the canteen; evenings spent playing cards in the company of a few close friends, or at Crockford's; making love, with rather cold passion, to one of three similarly disposed married women; week-ends playing golf for high stakes at one of the clubs near London.

One of the few women who "get away" from Bond is the lesbian Tilly Masterson (*Goldfinger*). She is killed in the attempt to capture Fort Knox, and Bond is there soon after she dies to pronounce the eulogy: "he said softly, 'Poor little bitch. She didn't think much of men'" (p. 240). For Bond as well as Fleming such sexual preferences were incomprehensible; if a woman would not go to bed with Bond, she was no doubt disturbed:

Bond came to the conclusion that Tilly Masterson was one of those girls whose hormones had got mixed up. He knew the type well and thought they and their male counterparts were a direct consequence of giving votes to women and "sex equality." As a result of fifty years of emancipation, feminine qualities were dying out or being transferred to the males. Pansies of both sexes were everywhere, not yet completely homosexual, but confused, not knowing what they were.

(p.221)

Consider Fleming's stereotyped treatment of women's bodies. From the first woman in his fictional life, Vesper Lynd, there is not much change. Vesper's hair is black, her eyes blue. Lightly suntanned, she wears no makeup (conforming to Fleming's preference for unaffected women who were as clean as possible). In contrast, Tilly Masterson makes no attempt to pat her hair into place; "as a result, it looked as a girl's hair should look—untidy, with bits that strayed and a rather crooked parting" (*Goldfinger*, p. 147). And Vesper's dress has a square-cut bodice, drawn "lasciviously tight across her fine breasts" (p 33). What are *fine* breasts? Later, when she and Bond are lovers, they turn out to be breasts that "filled his hands," whose "nipples were hard against his fingers" (p. 155).

One of the first things Bond notices about Solitaire is her long evening dress of heavy white matte silk, which is draped off her shoulders revealing the upper half of her breasts (*Live and Let Die,* p. 61). Later, when they become lovers, Fleming wants to tell us that Bond felt her hard breasts, "each with its pointed stigma of desire" (p. 97). Tiffany Case wears black, which James loves, especially against a sunburned skin. When Tiffany bends over to allow Bond to light her cigarette, "the valley between her breasts deepened" (p. 69). Later, at a restaurant, when he is shown to his table, Bond notices that she was showing him that at least the upper part of her breasts were real (p. 132).

Even when Bond does not get to sleep with the woman—and that is infrequent enough—Fleming cannot resist a stereotyped description of her. Gala Brand, for instance. Working undercover as Hugo Drax's administrative assistant, Bond reads in her official police record that she had a 38–26–38 figure with a mole on the upper curvature of her right breast as her sole distinguishing mark (p. 90). One may wonder what kind of police file this is. She is wearing a wrapover bodice when Bond meets her (p. 97), and it just showed "the swell of her breasts, which were as splendid as Bond had guessed from the measurements on her record sheet." Gazing at Drax's rocket, she might have been a schoolgirl looking at a Christmas Tree, but for "the impudent pride of jutting breasts" (p. 129). During one of the times off, down by Dover beach, Bond can not keep his mind (or his eyes) off "the pointed hillocks of her breasts" (p. 143). But this one gets away.

In *From Russia, with Love,* Red Grant, in the opening chapter, receives a message from a "girl" with nothing on under her shirt, whose skin was pleasantly sunburned, and whose "fine breasts" shone with health (p. 5). Tatiana has fallen in love with James from seeing a picture of him—something like the way in which Tristan falls in love with Isolde—and he is smitten with her looks, particularly the contrast between the innocence of her blue eyes and the sensuality of her mouth. He wonders about her virginity but decides that she must be experienced because "there was the confidence of having been loved in the proud breasts and the insolent lilting behind—the assertion of a body that knows what it can be for" (p. 145).

Bond's first sight of Honeychile Rider is pure wish-fulfillment fantasy. He is hiding on Dr. No's beach where Honeychile lands naked, except for a leather belt around her waist. Of course she is young and exceptionally beautiful, and from his hiding place Bond is able to observe her at his leisure—and pleasure. She had a beautiful back, a "behind almost as firm and rounded as a boy's," straight and beautiful legs. Her soles are not pink—"she was not a coloured girl" (p. 80). And, of course, she has "beautiful firm breasts that now jutted toward him without concealment" (p. 82).

Tilly Masterson (*Goldfinger*, p. 147) "held her body proudly—her fine breasts out-thrown and unashamed under the taut silk." But she turns out to be one of the confused ones, and she dies, conveniently, near the end. Pussy Galore has been a lesbian until she meets Bond; his genuine maleness converts her. Making love, on the last page of *Goldfinger*, Bond puts his right hand on her right breast (Fleming specifies "right" in both instances) and "its point was hard with desire." Domino Vitali (*Thunderball*, p. 181) gets similar treatment: "Bond closed his hand firmly over her right breast." She is on her back on the sand, the "mounded V" of her bikini thrust toward Bond, "and the proud breasts in the tight cups were two more eyes." Tracy Vicenzo, wearing "some kind of a plain white dress," blue-eyed and blond-haired, attracts Bond's notice (in *On Her Majesty's Secret Service,* p. 26) when she bends down, revealing "a moment of discrete cleavage." We know that she is something special when, a little later, Bond "put one hand firmly on the little hill that was her left breast" (p. 30). Meanwhile, there are diversions. Having breached Piz Gloria, Blofeld's mountain sanitarium, in disguise, Bond is introduced to the other guests—who are, unknown to him at that moment, Blofeld's victims: ". . . all he saw was a sea of beautiful, sunburned faces and a succession of splendid, sweatered young bosoms" (p. 71).

And so it goes. Let Tracy's reaction to Bond on their first night in bed represent Fleming's ideal of a sexual partner. She says to James: "Make love to me. You are handsome and strong. I want to remember what it can be like. Do anything you like. And tell me what you would like and what you would like from me. Be rough with me. Treat me like the lowest whore in creation. Forget everything else. No questions. Take me" (p. 30). After their lovemaking—which she says was "heaven. . . . I must have it once more," he takes a cold shower. She turns out to be one of the few women who interest Bond, and at the end of the book they marry. (To save Bond for further adventures, Fleming has her killed off by Blofeld a few hours after the wedding.) But while he will eventually find her interesting enough to marry, Bond's first reaction is significant: "What the hell? All cats are grey in the dark" (p. 31).

Fleming's attitude toward women is perhaps best shown in evaluations of their intelligence. In a moment of pique (in *Casino Royale*) Bond curses "these blithering women who thought they could do a man's work. Why the hell couldn't they stay at home and mind their pots and pans and stick to their frocks and gossip and leave men's work to the men? . . . The silly bitch" (p. 99). (The object of these remarks is also a secret agent.) When he makes out his report to "M," he charitably makes light of Vesper's "amateurish behavior" (p. 147). Tatiana complains vacuously that since she has left Russia she is "all stomach." She begs James not to let her get too fat: "You won't let me get so fat that I am no use for making love? You will have to be careful, or I shall just eat all day long and sleep" (p. 219). But she is safe from a life of bon bons and Bridge, thank God. Nevertheless, when Bond realizes that there is a plot afoot and he is its target, he considers her "a silly idiot" (p. 229).

Driving is said to have been one of Bond's passions, as it was Fleming's. This, too, is a talent that seems to belong almost exclusively to men. "Women are often meticulous and safe drivers, but they are very seldom first-class." That is the narrator talking. "In general Bond re-

garded them as a mild hazard and always gave them plenty of road and
was ready for the unpredictable. Four women in a car he regarded as
the highest danger potential, and two women as nearly as lethal.
Women together cannot keep silent in a car, and when women talk
they have to look at each other's faces. . . . So two women in the front
seat of a car constantly distract each other's attention from the road
ahead and four women are more than doubly dangerous, for the driver
has to hear, and see, not only what her companion is saying but also,
for women are like that, what the two behind are talking about" (p.
105).

   In *Goldfinger* Jill Masterson is the requisite bimbo. In the villain's
hire, she spies on outdoor canasta games with binoculars and tells her
boss by radio (concealed as his hearing aid) what cards are in the other
player's hand. When Bond breaks in on her in Goldfinger's hotel room,
she is sitting on some cushions just inside the open balcony door. She
is wearing only a black brassiere and black silk panties (this is a James
Bond adventure, after all), swinging her legs in a bored fashion. She
has just finished painting the nails of one hand when Bond enters,
silently, and is holding it in front of her, blowing on the wet lacquer
(p. 36). In one of Fleming's most redundant comments, he remarks
that "her breasts thrust against the black silk of the brassiere" (p. 37).
Do we have to be told this? Of course her breasts would thrust against
her brassiere; that is what the garment is for. But the obvious gets
mentioned here because Fleming wants to mention "breasts" and
"black silk brassiere" since that is what passes for sensuality in his
writing.

   Honeychile Rider is Fleming's archetypal fantasy ingenue, an ideal
target for Bond's admiring condescension, though her naivete also
evokes a patronizing respect for her innocence of his evil world. He
reflects that she has had to defend herself against natural enemies, "animals and insects and fishes," but that she is ignorant of the real world
of smoke-filled rooms, of careful meetings on park benches, of the
struggle for big power and big money waged by big men. He tells her,
"It's all right, Honey. They're just a lot of bad men who are frightened
of us" (*Doctor No,* p. 94). Why was he on the island at all? she soon
wants to know; "Bond told the story in simple terms, with good men
and bad men, like an adventure story out of a book" (p. 111). When
all of the shooting has ceased, Bond tells her that she is "one of the
most wonderful girls [he has] ever known." He considers telling her
about the real world, out "there." But she does not want to hear about

it—only about the pleasant things: "Now you can start telling me about love. Everything about it. Everything you know" (p. 230). Fleming could not have created a woman more directly from his own fantasies, or more immediately expressive of them.

Italian critic Furio Colombo sees in Bond's women a symbol of the "stake in the game." The "right" women, the desirable, well-bathed women are sooner or later to be found in bed with Bond. The others, such as Rosa Klebb or Irma Bunt (the ugliness of their names gives away their moral situation) illustrate the wickedness, the "scant charms," of the enemy. The Bond girl, Colombo thinks, is free, tenacious, combative, and yet sweet; her sexuality has been repressed since infancy (or early adolescence). Hers is an innocence without virginity— a type, as it happens, that was popular during the depression. Her descendant during the 1950s was the *Vogue* and *Esquire* "pal-girl" (in Eco, pp. 87–99).

Throughout the Bond novels women are prey for the predatory hero. Bond assumes this relationship to be ever operative. A detached woman is, by her very existence, a challenge to him. Vesper Lynd "gazed candidly back at Bond with a touch of ironical disinterest which, to his annoyance, he found he would like to shatter, roughly" (*Casino Royale,* p. 33). Some women, like Tracy, want Bond to treat them roughly. Some want to be cared for, like Solitaire, who understands that her life with Bond is going to be difficult and dangerous: "So will you please take good care of us?" (*Live and Let Die,* p. 87). Secret agent Tatiana Romanova, chosen by the KGB for a key role in the assassination of Bond, quickly falls in love with him. As the plot develops, her greatest fear turns out to be the fear of losing Bond—"this man who had suddenly become the light of her life" (*From Russia, with Love,* p. 206). So, too, Domino (in *Thunderball*), who tells him that "You're the first man who's ever made me cry" (p. 182).

But Colombo also notes that near the end of the Bond novels—or at the very end—the girl recedes toward nothingness, leaving James free of responsibility (p. 102). An ideal situation for a man whose sexual life has been seduce-and-run—the pattern of both Fleming and Bond. No foreign entanglements, no lasting relationships that would tie down the male lead and inhibit his activity (i.e., his sex life). The woman is enjoyed and then fades away. "Women," Bond says in *Casino Royale* (p. 28), "were for recreation. On a job, they got in the way and fogged things up with sex and hurt feelings and all the emotional baggage they carried around. One had to look out for them and take care of them." In Fleming's ideal world there were no complicating entanglements; women would be used and then left on their own to fend for themselves. "Bond saw luck as a woman, to be softly wooed or brutally ravaged, never pandered to or pursued" (p. 42).

This attitude is a constant throughout Bond's life. He feels a growing warmth toward Solitaire (*Live and Let Die,* p. 107) "and his desire for her body were in a compartment which had no communicating door with his professional life." Kerim Darko (*From Russia, with Love*) remarks to Bond that there is only one way of telling whether a woman really loves you, and that must be fathomed by an expert; "'Yes,' said Bond dubiously. 'I know what you mean. In bed'" (p. 124). Tatiana lovingly obliges. Bond, the expert, is most of the time in doubt about her intentions; her eyes "told him nothing except that the girl was happy, and that she wanted him to love her, and that she was surprised at what was happening to her" (p. 177).

In *Doctor No* Bond's mind-set is the same. After meeting Honeychile Rider during his first day on Dr. No's island, he tries to go to sleep that night but "his mind was full of the day and of this extraordinary Girl Tarzan who had come into his life. It was as if some beautiful animal had attached itself to him" (p. 120). In one of the last novels, *On Her Majesty's Secret Service,* James has penetrated Blofeld's Piz Gloria in the guise of Sir Hilary Bray, heraldic expert invited by the villain to establish his lineage. Ruby, one of the other patrons at the sanitarium, comes to James's room, giggling. What to do? Bond needs some time to do genealogical research—part of the job, after all—but he cannot let such an opportunity pass: "He gave her another long and, he admitted to himself, extremely splendid kiss, to which she responded with an animalism that slightly salved his conscience. 'Now then, baby.' His right hand ran down her back to the curve of her behind, to which he gave an encouraging and hastening pat. 'We've got to get you out of here'" (p. 98).

Other women, like Solitaire, will have nothing to do with men (*Live and Let Die,* p. 88)—until they meet Bond, of course. Tiffany Case first responds to Bond with seeming indifference (*Diamonds Are Forever,* p. 37); alone with him later, however, "she kissed him once hard and long on the lips, with a fierce tenderness that was almost without sex" (p. 73). On their first night of passion together she confides to Bond that "I've never what you call 'slept with a man' in my life" (p. 186).

Honeychile Rider has had a traumatic first sexual experience and wants to keep her life free of men (paradoxically, since she later tells Bond that to raise money for her nose operation she wants to be a big-city call girl), but the handsome Englishman turns out to be an exception, nothing at all like the others who so put her off. And so it is with Tracy, whom Bond sizes up as an unhappy girl who had "gone the route" (Bond's phrase); they have fulfilling sex, fall in love, and are even married, though just for a few hours. Fleming cannot give them everything, after all.

Bond's women—the desirable ones, anyway—are what Fleming thought women ought to be ideally. They should be loving; caring; beautiful with firm, athletic, sensual bodies; innocent but not virginal; impulsive enough to give themselves to Bond almost at first meeting, but chary of their favors with other men; ready to commit themselves to him but cheerfully willing to break off any relationship at his whim. Bond is made to reflect at one point (as remembered by a Fleming admirer, O. O. Snelling, p. 32) that if he ever did get married it would be to an "air hostess"; they are always "tucking you up" and bringing you hot meals, "And they're always smiling and wanting to please." His second choice would be a Japanese woman: "They seem to have the right idea idea, too." Intelligence is an indifferent trait in women— Fleming always had doubts about women's rational capacities—not to be admired and so, in the fiction, almost never mentioned, so long as they are not stupid enough to obstruct the hero's plans. They must not deter Bond from his professional duties or hinder him in his chosen course of action. They must make no incursions into his emotions. They exist, in short, to be used sexually (as Fleming has Bond declare explicitly on more than one occasion) and then discarded as the male sees fit. Affection is hard to find on Fleming's pages. Even Bond's lovemaking is described with a cold, hard cruelty. It seems to have been a bloodless exercise on Fleming's part, an activity that may have bolstered his self-confidence, but which is hard to imagine was emotionally fulfilling in any profound way. Despite Fleming's dwelling on sex, the aspect of his novels for which he became most famous (notorious?), it was an aspect of human interaction that he could not convincingly depict.

No further demonstration is necessary to show that what is true of Bond's feelings about women was also true of Fleming. After his mother broke up his romance with his Swiss fiancée, he vowed to use women in the future without scruple. Until he met Ann, they were not real human beings to him, not to be treated with the respect with which one treated equals. And after his marriage had soured, he seems to have enveloped Ann with many of his feelings that he had formerly felt about other women. When he discovered that even his relationship with Ann contained all of the pitfalls that he had imagined to be true when one was committed to a women, he blamed her, of course. But, in any case, it was too late.

It is difficult to project back to the English public's mood of the 1950s with great accuracy. Would Fleming's readers have been insensitive to his and James Bond's attitudes toward women and non-English ethnic groups? Judging from reviews of the Bond novels, racism and sexism were not pressing issues. Fleming's biases do not seem to have been too far out of the step with his readership in Great Britain. If this is true, then the public, especially the American public, has changed, and changed to Fleming's detriment. Six hundred years after the event, Chaucer scholars can protest that his character the Prioress, not Chaucer himself, was anti-Semitic. Fleming can have no such apologists. He felt that the English "race" was superior to all the other inferior groups, and that women were definitely subordinate to men. Those feelings appear in his writing unmistakably and unarguably. Fleming's supporters can only reply that the reader does not care, or that racism is acceptable.

When Fleming extols the racial purity of English white men, his thoughts are—as already noted—in the tradition of Sapper and John Buchan. Jews, for instance, in the novels of both of these writers, are less than human. Acquaintances of Fleming tell us that he shared the anti-Semitic bias of contemporary polite society. His attitudes toward women, however, did not come from his reading; they are Fleming's own, expressive not so much of societal values but of his private feelings about women and their place in his life.

Distancing himself from women and from "wogs" also kept Fleming from being swallowed up by them. Race prejudice is related to paranoia; one abhors what one is fearful of becoming. Bond knows that because he is Scottish he is different, that in England his Scottishness is difficult to cover up. Fleming the Scot was also conspicuous. Furthermore, Fleming was not one of those Englishmen (like D. H. Lawrence) who thought that racial others had some pipeline to the profound secrets of life; he does not seem to have doubted that his way and the English way were the noblest and best, and he did not want to contaminate that purity. He could keep the "wogs"—and women—in their place. Racial prejudice also saved him the mental strain of having to evaluate each person on his own merits; categorical judgments are always easier. Fleming took that route, adhering to the hierarchy that underlies every prejudicial attitudinal system: the English were the chosen race and men the favored gender. James Bond was the champion of that philosophy.

Chapter Eight
Fleming's Villains

Was it modesty or the stance of the Etonian gentleman that led Fleming to call Bond a "cardboard booby" and to denigrate the other characters in *Casino Royale* as banal? Whichever interpretation one gives to Fleming's motivations, the dreary fact of his dull characterization remains. Even his staunch supporter Kingsley Amis finds Bond "extremely dull" (p. 27). Did Fleming really say, as Amis claims, "How could I write such piffle?" (p. 128). Most of the characters may be nonentities, but that blanket condemnation does not apply to the villains (though Sauerberg, [p. 131] thinks that the adversaries are usually "flatter" than the hero). They are imposing titans, enlarged in some demoniacally spiritual way (though usually shorter than Bond physically)—perhaps because, if Bond was to gain and hold our admiration, he would need "a more than life-size figure" to overthrow (Amis, p. 56). And Fleming's villains *are* bigger than life; they are the characters we remember most vividly after we put down a Fleming novel.

When Fleming thought up Le Chiffre he had not quite got the hang of portraying evil. Pearson feels that the heavy of *Casino Royale* never becomes a genuine character, that he is a "sort of Identikit figure assembled out of a number of physical characteristics that Fleming seems to have found repellent or terrifying in people he had known" (p. 197). But every writer constructs his plot and characters out of his/her experience. Laura Lilli (in Eco, p. 155), comments that Le Chiffre is much like a stern parent. When he is punishing Bond and trying to torture information out of him—in that famous scene is which he beats Bond's genitals with a cane carpetbeater—he seems to be as regretful as a concerned parent who is pained more than the pain he inflicts: "'You see, dear boy?' He smiled a soft, fat smile. 'Is the position quite clear now?'" (*Casino Royale*, p. 113). And again:

"My Dear boy"—Le Chiffre spoke like a father—"the game of Red Indians is over, quite over. You have stumbled by mischance into a game for grown-ups, and you have already found it a painful experience. You are not equipped, my dear boy, to play games with adults, and it was very foolish of your nanny in London to have sent you here with your spade and bucket. Very foolish indeed, most unfortunate for you."

(p. 113)

It takes no great interpretive powers to see Le Chiffre as a father figure in this passage. But exactly how should we read it? As Fleming's own father (whom he barely knew) or as a masculinized version of that punitive parental figure, Fleming's mother? The scene is also redolent of the prefect's punishment room in British schools, and while Ian may have been punished severely in such chambers—especially considering what we know about his troublesome nature—there is no evidence that any prefect's corporal punishment left the kind of scars this scene seems to suggest. We do not think such readings are absurd, but we nevertheless want to give this scene a plainer reading; Le Chiffre is trying to humiliate Bond, to reduce his sense of self-esteem, and so he therefore addresses him as a child, trying to convince him that he is out of his element in the big world of adults. And in that world, children who do not know how to take care of themselves get hurt.

Seconds later he tells Bond that he is not living a romantic adventure story in which the noble hero defeats the villain, is widely acclaimed, and marries the princess. Those things, Le Chiffre assures the bound Bond, do not happen in "real life." If James persists in his refusal to reveal the location of the money, he will "be tortured to the edge of madness"; then Vesper will be brought in "and we will set about her in front of you"; and if that is not enough, they both will be "painfully killed" (p. 114). But Bond is up to the task. Silently he musters his psychic strength and refuses to comply with his torturer's demands. He is the hero who will not give in to his tormentor's evil demands for information. He is the schoolboy who will not capitulate to father or headmaster—perhaps.

The agency files describe Le Chiffre as five feet eight inches tall, eighteen stone in weight, with a "very pale" complexion and red-brown hair. His eyes are "very dark brown with whites showing all around iris" (p. 14 ff.). His mouth is small, almost feminine. He has expensive false teeth; his small ears with their large lobes "indicate Jewish blood," though he is probably a racial mixture of "Mediterranean with Prussian or Polish strains." He dresses well and meticulously, generally (odd touch for an official document) in "dark double-breasted suits." He smokes filtered Caporals incessantly. Both his English and his

French are fluent, and his German is good. He smiles infrequently and never laughs.

This file, like all the others in the Bond books, is both realistically factual and eccentric, so that we think of it and them as "Fleming-esque." Do the ears really suggest "Jewish blood" to the preparers of the agency's files? Can his "incessant" smoking—even the brand name is given—be an important trait? Can it be useful to know that his habits are "mostly expensive," though discreet; that he has "large sexual appetites" (compared to Bond?); that he is a "flagellant"? Like Bond, Le Chiffre drives fast cars and excels in various forms of personal combat, from small arms to knives. He carries "three eversharp razor blades" on his person. His "knowledge of accountancy and mathematics" no doubt contributes to his being a "fine gambler."

For our analysis of Fleming and his villains, only a few of these details are important. We should note, because it is a recurring trait, the red hair; several of Fleming's villains have it—Red Grant, Drax, Goldfinger. Red is Satan's color; but we are not willing to swear that this fact is relevant regarding Fleming's bad men. The racial descriptions are more germane. Do small ears with large lobes indicate "Jewish blood"? And would such a comment appear on a secret service profile, even in race-conscious England? A villain in the best tradition of Buchan and Sapper, Le Chiffre first appears as a stateless person at the Dachau Displaced Person's camp in 1945; his racial background, subsequently determined, is Mediterranean and Prussian or Polish.

Following such an introduction, however, Le Chiffre fails to live up to his promise. After pinning Bond to the ropes in the Casino, our villain has a major reversal of his luck and snatches defeat out of the jaws of certain victory. Later on comes the carpetbeater torture of Bond, with its condescending father-to-child monologue. Little else, however, is fascinatingly evil about him. Le Chiffre is not demonic, and not particularly memorable. Aside from beating Bond's bared genitals, Le Chiffre does little of interest—and that bit of sadism is not enough to immortalize him. In the end he dies at the hands of his own people, a hit squad sent out to punish him for losing SMERSH's funds at the gambling table. Though his characterization is more vivid than that of Bond himself, he turns out to be one of the most quickly forgotten of Fleming's villains. Bond reflects on the nature of good and evil after his encounter with Le Chiffre; the reader may not have such metaphysical thoughts.

Fleming followed Le Chiffre with Mr. Big (in *Live and Let Die*), the black gangster form Harlem. He is more interesting than Le Chiffre, but perhaps Fleming felt that a Negro would not be accepted by English readers in the 1950s as a plausible villain for more than one novel. More likely, it had not occurred to him to pit Bond in an ongoing struggle against one archfiend, like Holmes against Moriarty, or Drummond against Carl Peterson—or later, Le Carré's Smiley against Karla. Fleming would correct that lack of continuity with the creation of Blofeld, who appears in *Thunderball, On Her Majesty's Secret Service,* and *You Only Live Twice.*

For whatever reason, in order to expand the scope of Mr. Big's evil, he is portrayed not merely as the ruthless head of a murderous black gang operating out of Harlem but, in "M's" estimation, as "the most powerful negro criminal in the world" (p. 16). He is not merely the head of the Black Widow Voodoo cult, but also—and primarily—a Soviet agent, a known member of SMERSH. His various rackets and multifarious gangster activities finance a good part of the Soviet espionage system in America. Now *that* is a villainy that readers who had lived with the tensions of the cold war could understand.

Fleming several times introduces Bond's antagonists to the reader in straightforward expository passages. Sometimes certain background details are contained in lectures given Bond by "M" or his various experts—on the economics of gold, or the production and distribution of diamonds, for instance. *Live and Let Die* is no exception; we get most of our information about Mr. Big in a briefing by "M" just before he launches Bond on his assignment. Fleming's villains are almost certain to be of mixed blood, and so is this Harlem hoodlum. African Negroes are unambitious and in general law-abiding, "M" thinks. Mr. Big's problem is that he was born in Haiti and "has a good dose"of French blood (p. 17). And he was trained in Moscow, too. "M" admits that the "Negro races" are beginning to prosper in all of the professions, so it is "about time" that "they" produced a criminal.

In New York Bond is briefed by CIA agents, but though Fleming has him reflect that they added little to his knowledge of Mr. Big, the reader gets a fuller image of the man. His real name is Buonaparte Ignace Gallia; his initials have given him his "Big" street name. The moniker came early to him because of his enormous bulk. When Bond meets him, he finds an awesome giant six and a half feet tall weighing over 280 pounds. He does not drink or smoke, but consumes women in quantity—sure sign of a villainous character. (But then what about Bond's sexual capacity?) And he suffers from a chronic heart disease that has in recent years given his skin a grayish tinge. Later, when Bond is captured by him, he is struck by the man's nearly round "great football of a head," twice the "normal" size (p. 55). His gray-black skin shines like the face of a week-old corpse in the river. He has no eyebrows or lashes; and his eyes are set so far apart that one can focus on only one at a time. Perhaps it was a mercy, for they are blazing, animal eyes, "not human" (p. 55).

Too much has been made, we think, of Fleming's alleged sadism. Rather, he seems to us to devise intricate and exotic forms of execution in order to demonstrate the villain's demonic creativity. Would not it be easier, less expensive, and surer to put a bullet through Bond's brain? Why bother with such rococo death schemes unless the villain's fiendish creativity is meant to be shown? On this score Le Chiffre is lacking; beating Bond's bared genitals is not meant to kill him, first of all, and as torture it is not as effective as acts prescribed in the Gestapo's manual—or that of the KGB for that matter. One should give Mr. Big his due; after recapturing Bond and his former mistress, Solitaire, he ties them, naked, to a tow-rope he intends to drag, at speed, over a coral reef. The idea is that the coral will lacerate both of them, and their blood will attract sharks and barracuda, whose feeding frenzy will finish the job for him. Bond and the woman will die hideous deaths. A bullet in the back of the neck would be too painless, and Fleming also wants (and likes) his villains to exact as much terror from their victims as possible before they die.

Fleming had several good ideas when he created Mr. Big. In a way, it is too bad that Bond successfully killed him off; he seems to be good for two or three further adventures. Unless, as we said before, Fleming decided that a Negro was not "right" for such an important villainous role.

Hugo Drax of *Moonraker* (his real name is Drache, "dragon") was an almost perfect villain, but he, too, is killed. Once again, "M" briefs Bond on Drax in early expository passages, but Sir Hugo is a celebrity in this fictional London, his only fault—and the reason for Bond's assignment—is that he is suspected of cheating at cards, during those eminently civilized games between members at Blades. So we have to wait until James reveals his cheating ways to realize, with certainty, that he is a bounder.

"M" is not certain about Sir Hugo's background, but he knows that he was caught in a raid by German commandoes (called "Werewolves") in 1944 and was among the English casualties; he was left with "half his face blown away" (p. 17). When Bond meets him, he finds a large man—about six feet tall—whose face has been incompletely restored by plastic surgery. English literary villains for centuries had been marked by physical deformities in some way; Fleming picked up on this device and used it almost unvaryingly. Like Mr. Big, Drax has a big head (this time square, not round), and like Le Chiffre his hair is reddish. Bond assumes that his part in the middle, enabling tufts of it to dip down toward the temples on either side, is an attempt to cover up the scarred tissue. The skin on the right half of his face is puckered and shiny. His ears do not match, and his right eye, owing to surgical failure, is larger than his left (p. 36).

Like other Fleming villains, Drax is not English. He is in some way German, though at the moment of the novel he is working for Russia (Eco comments: "Communist-Nazi," p. 45). Drax's credentials as a villain are impeccable. He is deformed, he is an alien, and he has red hair. When Bond has been captured, near the end of the adventure, and serves as a captive audience for Sir Hugo's anti-English diatribe, the picture is completed. He tells Bond that he is not English, that during 1944 he was operating behind Allied lines and wearing an English uniform, he rode into a rear area depot and hospital and blew it up. Escaping, still in a British uniform, he was strafed on the road by a Luftwaffe plane, thus receiving his grievous wounds—not in an English hospital, as "M" had thought. In the hospital, he plotted his revenge on England and the English, for whom he feels nothing but hatred and scorn. The English are too weak to defend their colonies, he says; they toady to America, hat in hand; they will do anything for money. Drax is sure that to gain status in England all he needs is money (pp. 195–98).

Now he has the means for revenge—his rocket, "Moonraker." Instead of using it for England's glory, he has set its gyros to have it land, atomic warhead and all, back in England. Drax and his workers, meanwhile, will escape to Russia by submarine. Like his villainous predecessors, Drax does not dispose of Bond properly—in the easy way. Instead he locks him and Gala Brand, his assistant who had been working for British Intelligence all along, in the missile silo, thinking to scorch them both to death when "Moonraker" lifts off. But Bond endures. He and Gala both escape, though for saving his country Bond must once again go in hospital, to emerge latticed with surgical tape. Miraculously, there is no radioactive residue from "Moonraker's" redirected flight and descent. The Empire is safe until *Diamonds Are Forever.*

And that adventure lacks a truly meaty villain. Bond goes undercover as a courier for a diamond smuggling operation and gets to travel to Sarasota, Las Vegas, New York, and the gang's headquarters in the desert, Spectreville. He meets, and of course seduces, Tiffany Case. But apart from the minor excitement of a railroad chase—Bond steals a locomotive to make his escape from his Spectreville captors—there are not many thrills in this thriller, and only minor-league villains. Perhaps because they are Americans, Jack and Seraffimo Spang are bland, and the lesser villains, Wint Kidd and Shady Tree, even blander. The Spangs' attempt to re-create the Wild West of the nineteenth century in Spectreville had comic possibilities, but Fleming passed most of them by. The Spangs are just not memorable. Those villainous qualities Fleming had seemed to be developing over the first three books have been forgotten here. Red Grant, the assassin in *From Russia, with Love,* is not a satisfactory villain either. He had red hair—always a sign of evil—and a red-brown face, and his very pale blue eyes were part of a face that communicated "blankness" (p. 8). But these are the only physiognomic hints we get of his wickedness. Fleming had to inflict him with lunar madness in order to make him genuinely and terrifyingly demonic. Grant is susceptible to full moons; when he was sixteen he went out on a particular full-mooned October night and killed a cat. After that he felt better for the whole month. In November he killed a large sheepdog, and a month later he slit the throat of a cow. This cycle of escalation climaxed when, a short distance from his home, he killed a sleeping tramp (pp. 15–16). His talents soon came to the attention of the Sinn Feiners, and then to the talent scouts of SMERSH, for whom he became a contract killer.

It is with his seventh Bond novel, *Goldfinger,* that Fleming creates a villain of major proportions. The Spangs might have been operatives of Russian Intelligence, but that connection was so deeply submerged beneath the reader's consciousness that it hardly seemed relevant. Goldfinger is an agent of SMERSH, and while that role is also not particularly germane to the action, he nevertheless steals all the scenes through the power of his own personality and becomes the center of our attention.

In his conception of the corporeal Goldfinger (all from pp. 28–29),

Fleming relied on traits that he had found effective in the past. Like Mr. Big, Auric Goldfinger has a "huge" and almost exactly round head; it is brown and red like a football, pretty much of the same simile used to describe Mr. Big. He wears his carroty hair (!) in a crew cut, and while he has no obvious deformities, his thick body and blunt peasant legs, his head set directly on top of his shoulders—so that he appears to have no neck—give Bond the feeling that he has been put together with scraps of other people's bodies: "Nothing seemed to belong." Bond reflects that it is the short men who have caused all the trouble in the world, from Napoleon through Hitler, and now Goldfinger— this "misshapen short man with red hair and a bizarre face." Goldfinger's parts add up to "a really formidable misfit."

Misfit he is, in his ethnic origins as well. Junius Du Pont, whom Bond agrees to help (Goldfinger has been cheating him at cards), thinks that Goldfinger might be Jewish, because of his name, but that he does not look it. Besides, the Du Ponts are staying at a "restricted" hotel where Jews are not allowed. Bond thinks, on first seeing this bizarre man, that while he is probably not a Jew, there might be Jewish blood in him. He came, Bond reasons, from "one of the old Baltic provinces," possibly to escape from the Russians. (Bond is wrong, of course; Goldfinger *works* for the Russians.) Eco has called Goldfinger "absolutely a textbook monster" (p. 43). We add, to Goldfinger's "textbook" evil, his monomaniacal passion for gold and things golden. And, in a technique that Fleming would quickly ritualize, Goldfinger is given several paragraphs in which he develops an apologia. He explains to Bond, "in a rather bored voice" (p. 173), that he is engaged upon "gigantic enterprises." A little later he announces to the captive Bond that he "is expert in many things besides metals" and that he has a keen appreciation of everything that is excellent to the degree of perfection" (p. 182). For the lower forms of humanity—such as his servant, Oddjob—he has little use. All of his life he has been in love— with gold (p. 184). But above all he loves the power that it can bring to the owner—controlling energy, exacting labor, fulfilling one's every wish and whim, even controlling minds and souls. And so he espouses any enterprise that will increase his supply of gold—investing, smuggling, stealing (p. 185).

This absolute monster is given an assistant who is almost the perfect model for the role. Oddjob, the lethal Korean who eats cats given him as rewards, has a cleft palate that encourages his silence at nearly all times; only Goldfinger can understand his garbled articulation. And the plot itself is worthy of such a monster—or perhaps our appreciation of him is heightened by the nature of his scheme. He will irradiate the gold in Fort Knox with a small atomic explosion, thus depriving the American government of its use. In the ensuing financial chaos, he, Goldfinger, will profit financially while SMERSH gains politically.

The eponymous Doctor No is one of Fleming's most creatively conceived characters. He is tall—at least six inches taller than Bond. His completely bald skull tapers to his narrow chin—an inverted drop of liquid, oil, as Bond would have it, so as to more closely describe his translucent yellow skin. Prominent cheekbones jut out above cavernous cheeks. His slanting, black eyes beneath lashless brows are like two pistols, "direct and unblinking, and totally devoid of expression" (*Doctor No,* p. 155). His "compressed wound of a mouth" (p. 155) shows only authority and cruelty. He glides around, a monstrous, venomous worm clothed in grey tin-foil. When he apologizes for not shaking hands with Bond, we see that Fleming has not forgotten to give him a deformity: he has no hands, and from his kimono's sleeves steel pincers protrude.

Dr. No's servants are mostly Chigroes, Chinese and Negro halfbreeds, one of whom, like Oddjob, "a short man . . . with the build of a wrestler" serves drinks (p. 156). No can summon this nameless bodyguard by a tiny radio transmitter that he keeps in the lapel of his kimono. He is, like Drax, a scientist. Like nearly all of Fleming's villains, he works for the Russians, but on a free-lance basis. His scheme in this novel is to send misleading information to American missiles in flight, instructing their guidance systems to land within his reach.

Doctor No's apologia, delivered to Bond and Honeychile (who is all the while sipping on a Coke), makes his mad evil plain to us as well. He was born of a German Methodist missionary and a Chinese "girl of good family" (p. 162), thus establishing his mixed ethnic heritage in the best tradition of Fleming's villains. When he was old enough he went to work with one of the Shanghai Tongs, where he "loved the death and destruction of people and things" (p. 162). The Tongs were his form of revolt against a hated father. To escape from "trouble" in Asia, he emigrated to America, joining another, also powerful Tong. Made treasurer of the Hip Sings, he fled with all of their cash when a Tong war descended into chaos. It "was a time of torture and murder and arson which [he] joined with delight" (p. 163).

The survivors of the Tong tracked No down and tortured him, hoping to make him reveal where he had cached the gold. When he would not tell, his hands were cut off. Then he was shot "through the heart";

but his torturers could not know that he was the one in a million whose heart was in the wrong place—on the right side of his body. He survived. When he got out of the hospital he bought rare stamps with his gold, thus securing a portable fortune. He patiently waited, then, for the stamps to appreciate with inflation and increased demand after the war. He changed his appearance to baffle the Tong. He had all of his hair taken out by the roots, his nose bobbed, his mouth widened and his lips "sliced." Weeks of spinal traction gave him greater height, and assiduous practice changed his carriage and his walk. Then he changed his name: it had been Julius after his father, but he dropped that and added "No" to show his rejection of his parent and of authority.

It was in Milwaukee, at the "Faculty of Medicine," that No devoted himself to the study of the human body and the human mind. He had wanted to inure himself from any kind of human weakness, "from material dangers and from the hazards of living" (p. 164). His ultimate desire was to be able to wield over others the power that had once oppressed him, "the power of life and death, the power to decide, to judge, the power of absolute independence from outside authority" (p. 165). When he left Milwaukee he bought Crab Key, the Caribbean island fortress where he has lived for fourteen years before Bond's unexpected and unwanted arrival. Finding the island rich in bird dung, he imported Chinese laborers to mine it, and ship it to nations needing fertilizer—for a handsome profit, of course. Once that business was thriving, he sought to expand his horizons. Being expert in electronics (and rich enough to hire experts in areas he had not yet mastered), he decided to intercept American missiles in flight and to bring them to ground within his possession. And that was his present occupation. But his hobby remained the testing of the performance of human beings. And so, in the interests of scientific inquiry, he would put Bond through an intricate torture, and stake out Honeychile in the path of carnivorous crabs, just to note their reactions.

But much of the potential for evil on Crab Key remains unfulfilled. Dr. No seems an ideal villain in many ways: his mixed ethnic origins, his striking features, his deformity, his background in crime ruthlessly perpetrated, his obsession with power, his manic apologia to his captives, his role as "mad scientist." He puts Bond to the test, enabling him to endure great suffering and emerge unbowed. Honeychile is untouched by the crabs, though we do not learn of her escape until after Bond has managed his own. But somehow we expect more of Dr. No. His evil is cosmic; it should not end on Crab Key, deluged under tons of falling guano. Although the mad scientist, updated for a world of

missiles and atomic warheads, has great possibilities, torturing Bond
is the only task Fleming gives him in this novel. The diversion of
missiles takes place off the page, as does No's appetite for arson and
murder. Killing him was a mistake. Dr. No is far too valuable a literary
property to throw away so easily. We must give Fleming high marks
for creating a demonic character so hauntingly sinister, but we regret
that he was never given a larger role to play in the fantasy world of
James Bond. Doctor No could have kept Bond going for several novels,
and we would have had the curiosity of learning of his new schemes.
Burial beneath a mound of bird dung is appropriate for this power-
hungry scientist—but it should have happened several novels later.

The idea of a continuing struggle between the champions of good
(England, the white race, capitalism) and evil did not materialize until
the creation of Ernest Stavro Blofeld, Bond's antagonist in *Thunderball,*
the eighth novel in the series. In this characterization Fleming has
definitely profited from experience; traces of several of his extant villains appear in the character of Blofeld. Fleming even includes in Blofeld's biography a detail of his own life: both men were born on 28
May 1908. The claim that Fleming's humor materialized in little jokes
with his readers gains support here. Or is this a joke that only a few
close friends (and Ann) could appreciate?

That detail aside, the Fleming formula for villainy runs true to form
so far as it goes, but in the later novels he is not concerned with including all the details. Some of them are mandatory, of course; Blofeld's heritage is mixed; born in Gdynia, his father is Polish and his
mother Greek. After graduation from the University of Warsaw and
the Warsaw Technical Institute, he worked in "a modest post" for the
Ministry of Posts and Telegraphs. Exploiting his access to official communications that passed through his office, he at first sold confidential
material to the Germans, then to the Swedes and the Americans. After
a short while the profits were enormous.

He invested his money lucratively and was able to immigrate to
Turkey before his native Poland fell. From there, with an espionage
network that he established (actually faked so as to impress his cus-
tomers), he further enriched himself, putting the money into a Swiss
bank. The war ended with heartfelt thanks from the Allies and half a
million dollars in Swiss banks. Blofeld emigrated again, this time to
South America. When he returned to Europe, independently wealthy,
it was to Paris. He had, Fleming tells us, "a superbly clear brain" that
had been honed by thirty years of successfully evaded danger, and a

confidence that came from a lifetime of success in whatever he tried (pp. 41–43).

Blofeld's face is large, white, and bland, his crew-cut black (not red) and wiry. Only his heavy, squat nose spoils what might otherwise be the face of a scientist or of a philosopher. Fleming is more subtle about his "deformity": "Proud and thin, like a badly healed wound, the compressed, dark lips, capable only of false, ugly smiles, suggested contempt, tyranny, and cruelty—but to an almost Shakespearian degree. Nothing about Blofeld was small" (p. 44). In middle age his once muscularly athletic two hundred and eighty pounds has turned to fat. His long and pointed hands and feet still retain their quickness, however. He does not smoke or drink (a bad sign?—Fleming and Bond did both) and has never been known to sleep with a partner of either sex (p. 44). All of his thoughts and all of his energies, including his psychic energies, are devoted to acquiring wealth and power, the aggrandizement of SMERSH, and the nurturing of evil. At the moment of the *Thunderball* adventure, Blofeld has gathered around him in an organizational meeting twenty of Europe's most brilliant yet corruptible minds. Physicists, electronics experts, criminals, espionage specialists, they came to him from Germany, Poland, the Sicilian Mafia, Corsica, Yugoslavia, Russia (former members of SMERSH); some are recent officers of the Gestapo. Each of these experts in conspiracy had a "solid cover," a valid passport, and a clean record both with Interpol and with their local police forces (p. 45).

When we meet him later in *You Only Live Twice* almost no further description is given. Having to make his way to Blofeld's island without notice, Bond sees this master of death dressed in chain mail, helmeted with a spiked steel plate, "something out of Wagner" or, because the island is in Asia, out of a Kabuki play. Blofeld's cohort is Irma Bunt, a "stumpy woman with the body and stride of a wardess" (p. 127). We met her before, in *On Her Majesty's Secret Service,* where she was just as ugly, just as squat, just as unfeminine. Once, when bending low to leave through a cabin door, "she bent low, her tight, squat behind inviting an enormous kick" (p. 67), but James wisely forbore. In her squatness, her ugliness, her evil disposition, she is the sister of Rosa Klebb, whose kick with a poisoned blade on her shoe nearly kills Bond in *Casino Royale.* She is grotesquely portrayed in her obscene attempt to seduce lovely Tatiana Romanova in *From Russia, with Love*: "Colonel Klebb opened her dumpy arms and twirled on her toes like a mannequin. She struck a pose with one arm outstretched and the other arm crooked at the waist" (p. 81). More explicitly, Fleming tells us a moment later that "she looked like the oldest and ugliest whore in the world" (p. 82).

Evil is recognizable in Fleming chiefly by its ugliness. In women villains—always evil assistants, never the source of evil power itself—this ugliness is manifest in fat, squatness, age, clumsiness. Klebb and Bunt are nothing like the young, nubile, and willing women whom we know as the Bond girls; in *From Russia, with Love* the ugly Rosa is directly contrasted with the lovely Tatiana, as in *On Her Majesty's Secret Service* the squat Irma is made all the uglier for her proximity to the lovelies in the Piz Gloria. Beautiful women may not be potent forces for good—only Bond and his male friends achieve that status—but they qualify as acceptable, though passive, embodiments of the Right. We know the Bond girls are Good because they are sensual, that Dr. No (for instance) is Bad because he is deformed; like all of Fleming's male villains, he is made ugly because of some deformity or other, and that aesthetic judgment is moral as well. It is almost as though Fleming believed that the body was a reflection of the soul—beautiful flesh and bones betokened good, deformity (in men) and departure from the current canons of beauty (in women) was a sign of evil, or at the very least of a disagreeable personality. Evil, in Fleming, is the will to power (or authority, or responsibility) that "properly" belongs to England or the English.

Whether or not Fleming's villains are extensions of a father figure is unclear. But certainly they embody racial inferiority, physical deformity, and an uncompromising dedication to fiendish works performed on behalf of an evil institution, the agencies of communism. Fleming was never able to make Bond or the women he sleeps with interesting. But his villains are memorable. Fleming's formula for evil—striking ugliness and deformity, monomaniacal commitment to a cause, however depraved—has given his villains a certain vitality. Richard Usborne has sagely observed that "authors, unless they are careful, fall in love with their big villains" (p. 182). With Dr. No, Goldfinger, and Blofeld (and Bunt), Fleming attained a level of literary portraiture higher than in much of his other writing.

Chapter Nine
Ian Fleming: The Final Report

Few writers in this century have angered their readers as much as Ian Fleming. In general, critics have taken offense at the ethics and morality of James Bond and, by extension, of his author. Nearly all of the critiques have been variations or elaborations of the "sex, snobbery, and sadism" charge of Paul Johnson (*New Statesman,* April, 1958). Not much has been written about Fleming's writing skills (or lack of them). In this chapter we summarize what we feel have been the most perspicacious analyses of his work—psychological, moral, and aesthetic.

His critics have not been calm and dispassionate. J. Kenneth Van Dover (1984) is one of the few who even bother to criticize Fleming's writing style, and that with more objectivity than many of his other detractors. Notice is made of Fleming's poor ear for dialect (p. 178), despite Raymond Chandler's putative praise for the dialect in *Live and Let Die.* The matter is controversial: Snelling thinks that these same Harlem characters are some of Fleming's finest, and that his "handling of urban negro dialect is . . . completely convincing" (p. 120). How racist are these books? Snelling argues that Bond's "most intimate" male friends were non-Caucasian: Tanaka, Kerim, Draco, Quarrel (p. 188). James can also unburden himself with Mathis (*Casino Royale*), and while he is Caucasian, he is also French. Not a "wog," of course, but nearly one (the British have a saying: "The wogs begin at Calais"). We think that Van Dover was right on both counts.

The fascination with "exotic" races has often accompanied the English interest in colonial peoples and those in the far reaches of the Empire, as Cawelti observes in *The Spy Story* (p. 96 ff.). In this respect Fleming's models are Buchan's Sandy Arbuthnot, Lawrence of Arabia, "Chinese" Gordon, etc. Following a suggestion of Freud's, Cawelti comments that overcivilized white men may feel that in exotic cultures there is something deep, something mystically profound that is missing from "civilized" life. The "wogs"—as D. H. Lawrence, for example, believed—experience life in deep ways that Westerners have lost because of their "hyper" civilization.

But we are hard put to find this yearning for simpler ways in Fleming's writing. His racial others are, for the most part, not objects of
envy. In this attitude, Fleming is very much the creature of his childhood readings in Sapper and in Buchan. For James Bond certain foreigners are "safe"; he can confide in them because they are outside of
civilized society. But racial others are not racial equals. Confidences
made to those others do not circulate among the "in-group"; thus out-
siders are ideal sounding boards, acquaintances to whom one can unburden oneself of heartfelt thoughts, and do so without fear of one's
feelings ever being known where it really counts, among one's own
people. David Holbrook (*The Mask of Hate,* p. 127) found in the Bond
novels a defensive maneuver on Fleming's part against recognition of
human weaknesses that would be exposed by intimate relationships—
such as marriage. Fleming was vulnerable and childish; Bond would
be strong and sophisticated. The fictional creation would be given mastery over a great deal of arcane lore of which his author was innocent.
As is well-known, Fleming exploited the knowledge of others—the
knowing phrase, the arcane fact, the brushed-on varnish of authority
(Holbrook, p. 128)—and often succeeding in convincing people that
this knowledge reflected his own expertise. The *London Times* (quoted
in Gant, p. 82), for example, thought *Live and Let Die* "an ingenious
affair, full of recondite knowledge and horrific spills and thrills."

Psychologist Anthony Storr (p. 20) finds in Bond's vast expertise the
compensatory quality of the secret agent as fantasy wish-fulfillment.
Bond is expert in the use of the firearms, a connoisseur of fine foods
and wines, a knowledgeable motorist, and a dedicated gambler. But
Fleming, Storr asserts, did not know much about guns or wines (he
usually drank either vodka or whiskey himself), was a cautious driver,
and seldom gambled at casinos. "Expertise, therefore, became something which fascinated Fleming: something which he himself could not
acquire, but which other men possessed," and which he wanted for
himself. He achieved these skills through Bond's possession of them.

Storr finds deeper longings in the important relationships in Fleming's life (pp. 17–21). Fleming's fatherless adolescence produced a profound, lifelong sense of inferiority. It is often difficult enough to grow
up in the shadow of one's real father; in Ian's case the father was seldom
there—and not at all after age eleven—and his virtues no doubt were
overemphasized, his faults overlooked. Storr thinks this is why Fleming was a hero-worshipper all of his life. At Eton, his first idol was his
brother Peter. After that he greatly cherished "Intrepid," Lord

Beaverbrook, his neighbor Noel Coward, and friend W. Somerset Maugham. Bond's hero was his chief in the Secret Service, the man known as "M."

Van Dover considers the extensive background material in *You Only Live Twice* uninteresting and unconvincing (p. 206), and Blofeld's villainy in *You Only Live Twice* inexplicable. But realism was never Fleming's strength. At another place (p. 182), Van Dover observes that Fleming's novels blend farce with melodrama, that he mixes fact with the ridiculous. Writers commonly conflate genres; Fleming is not distinctive in this respect. But, it is true, his conflations do not seem to be carefully fashioned. Bond, the bureaucratic government agent (for instance), working away for months at a time in a stuffy office with his secretary and his blue suit, is suddenly thrust into the midst of the most incredible adventures. Science fictions, his adventures have been called—or comic strips for the upper middle classes (in Gant, p. 82). How are we to respond to a protagonist surrounded by innumerable facts and immersed in the details and brand names of everyday modern life, who acts out the most improbable scenarios? Is he a realistic hero, or one of fantasy? In what world does James Bond really live? In a sophisticated reading of the Bond novels, Cawelti (*The Spy Story,* p. 131) sees humor and self-irony, "the feeling of not taking it all too seriously, which makes it easier for sophisticated modern readers to give themselves up to the fantastic world of heroic adventure." Nevertheless, many readers are uncertain how to respond to Fleming.

David Holbrook (*The Mask of Hate*), unhappy with the social and psychological effects of the Bond novels (a common enough response), devastatingly attributes them to Fleming's personality. He begins with a critique of Fleming's style, focusing on *Goldfinger.* Cliché-ridden, it gives no "inward feel of the experiences of human beings in action or danger" (p. 68). Holbrook finds Fleming's action "at the level of a boy's adventure paper" (p. 67), his prose that of boy's adventure stories (p. 69). The novel is "tedious" and "boring" (p. 67). *The Masks of Hate* pronounces Fleming a paranoid, and his prose paranoid-schizoid, expressing "anxiety over a situation . . . involving a threat to the ego" (p. 70). His depersonalization of sex is a "manifestation of flight from life" (p. 71). Storr notes that Fleming's initial response to failure was not to try harder but rather to retreat into fantasy (p. 19). Fleming responded in this way to failures at Eton and Sandhurst, his performance on the Foreign Office exam, his brief careers as a journalist, banker, and stockbroker.

Fleming could find no essential integrity in himself and no essential value in others. Thus, Holbrook concludes, Bond's behavior is "virtually psychopathological" (p. 108). The secret agent's recurring concern with what is right is a "self-defensive defence mechanism" concerned with ego-preservation as well as a sign of contempt for others. Many of the scenes of violence show a detached yet aggressive Bond overcoming his (and his author's) fear of inner weakness (p. 109). Fleming's personal rituals—according to Holbrook, who has studied the author's life as well as his books—detached him from human company (p. 124). Ann Fleming once wrote (quoted in Amory, pp. 126–27): "There was something defensive and untamed about him. . . . Ian liked me because I amused him . . . and made no real demands on him." On this point she was perceptive.

Holbrook concludes that Fleming saw sex with a small boy's imagination of what he will be able to achieve as a man (p. 69). His women are objects for the taking (p. 77). They must also be kept under control, and thus are not allowed to be human (p. 115). Concentrating again on *Goldfinger,* Holbrook sees in its sexual scenes a disguised homosexuality (p. 78); in the invented acronym, SMERSH, a blending of "smash," "merge," *"mere," "merde"*—or, in other words, a paranoid-schizoid sadistic fantasy (p. 78).

No one ever became a lesbian by being seduced by her uncle, as Pussy Galore claims; yet we are asked to believe that this assault on her girlhood chastity accounts for her preference for Bond at *Goldfinger*'s conclusion. In Fleming's uncomplicated world, a lesbian is simply a woman who fails to respond to Bond. The "challenge" that a lesbian seems to pose to the hero's virility hides Fleming's "underlying primitive phantasy" (p. 101). Holbrook finds in Ms. Galore a projection of Fleming's "unconscious homosexuality" (p. 101). Bond's great sexual activity is a compensatory act for his fear of homosexuality (p. 112). Fleming's suppressed feelings for men—in this interpretation—and his heightened heterosexual activity (and Bond's) is actually a flight from his (their) own feminine element, and from his own feelings of hatred of women (p. 132).

For James Bond, the safety of his ego is the only consideration (p. 136). Holbrook finds in the Bond novels an intense hatred of women (a view that would be supported in Fleming's biography), the other side of which is fear of his own female element (p. 100). His sexual activity is depersonalized, enabling him to remain detached, uninvolved, thus protecting his vulnerability. Fleming could find no essential integrity in himself, and no essential human value in others. Bond's world, as we have seen, is entirely one of objects to be consumed or destroyed. Feeling a threat to his inner contents in marriage, Fleming wrote as a defence against those contents being taken away from him (pp. 130–31). The mythology of the spy was for him based on an intense need to preserve those inner contents—through this paranoidal reaction. Bond's behavior is, for these reasons, "virtually psychopathological" (p. 108).

His relations with women—as have been many times commented upon—were not love relations; Anthony Storr (pp. 19 ff.) thinks that they were motivated by a will to power. Both Bond and Fleming went in for conquests, proofs of masculinity that lacked tenderness and commitment. Though they may not seem insurmountable to outside observers, Fleming's failures were devastating to him; so, as he translated his life experiences into fiction, he would feel that if Bond could not succeed as a man, he could at least suffer like one. Storr also notes Fleming's obsessions with power and wealth—things that other men possessed and that he craved. His villains had the power and wealth that Fleming himself craved (p. 20). Goldfinger would no doubt be the exemplar of the greedy man, with Drax, Blofeld, and Dr. No running as neck-and-neck seconds. Their power is expressed in the control they have over the lives of others, in their technological mastery, and their delight in cruelty for its own sake.

Bond has also had his supporters, and they have not been psychologically or morally oriented but more conventionally literary. The most famous of these is Kingsley Amis (*The James Bond Dossier*), who both grants Fleming's faults ("Nobody could call Mr. Fleming a profound writer . . . ," p. 122) and praises him lavishly for traits that others have criticized. Amis grants that Fleming's Harlem and gangster slang are obsolete "mistakes" (p. 111). Bond's friend Felix Leiter is a "nonentity as a piece of characterization" (p. 78), and Bond himself is "extremely dull, uninteresting" (p. 27). Amis also admits that Fleming's writing is riddled with dangling participles, mixed metaphors, and trite passages (p. 123). And, finally, he admits that human relations "get a poor showing" (p. 125).

But Amis does find positive virtues in the Bond books, though his standards and comparisons are not always impeccable. He believes, for instance, that the sexual interpretations of Bond's sufferings are a mistake; he then cites similar adventures of Bulldog Drummond, who was also several times captured but who also escaped without being seriously tortured (p. 13). The usual "Bond-girl," he observes, has "fine," "firm," "faultless," "splendid" etc., breasts, but what would be a better focus, Amis wonders—"a girl's feet, perhaps?" (pp. 44–45).

Amis concedes that, in the Bond books, it does not matter what one does as long as it is done for the right side; and, to demonstrate this point, Amis again cites (by way of contrast) Bulldog Drummond—who once dropped the villain into an acid bath. In this world, skewering with bayonets is also OK (p. 72). On racism, Amis lists Fleming's villains: Bulgars, Corsicans, Germans, Italians, Yugoslavs, Koreans, Russians, Sicilians, Turks, Spanish-Americans, Chigroes, and Americans. But it should be noted that in Sapper and G. K. Chesterton the baddies are Poles, Germans, Russians, Jews—the collective "dago"—and all of them are undesirable aliens (pp. 74–75). American readers especially may wonder if these comparisons are finally to Fleming's credit.

Amis admires Fleming's novels because he has imprinted on them "his stamp . . . of action and intrigue, bringing to it . . . a power and a flair that will win him readers when all the protests about his supposed deficiencies have been forgotten" (p. 132). What American readers in particular would see as racism, sexism, and adolescent male chauvinism, Amis finds in the mainstream of English boyhood adventure writing. Bond was a patriot when the Empire was melting away as surely as the Englishmen's pride in his country, when the public needed competent patriots. Like Buchan, Sapper, and Yates, Fleming extolled the virtues of the Anglo-Saxon, while denigrating other races and nationalities. Amis finds this wholesome and appropriate fare for Fleming's audience. And, as for Bond's women, Amis finds them appealing, suitably described, and has no personal objections to an occasional roll in the hay. Traveling salesmen also do it.

O. F. Snelling's *Double O Seven James Bond: A Report* treats its subject more as a man of real life than of fiction: "I sleep a lot easier at night now I know that men like Bond are around" (p. 127). Much of the book is a descriptive catalog of Bond's traits, whims, and habits; he spends his leisure time playing cards, making love, driving fast cars; he smokes sixty cigarettes a day, more when under tension; he distrusts men who tie windsor knots; he himself always wears blue suits, sea-island shirts, and black knitted ties; and he likes his girls to clip their fingernails short (pp. 23, 26, 37, 46).

But Snelling has an opinion on Fleming the writer as well. An "accomplished yarn-spinner" (p. 43), he could "paraphrase the telephone book and still be readable" (p. 55). Next to Thomas Wolfe, Snelling finds, Fleming wrote the most excellent descriptions of "delectable food" (p. 28). In *Thunderball,* "we have a magnificent work of the imagination" (p. 88). On characterization: Ian Fleming is the phenomenon he is . . . primarily because of the subtle character-drawing. We are carried along in his books because we believe in his people, no matter what outlandish tricks they may get up to" (p. 87). In *Thunderball* (again) "we get little of that engaging character-drawing . . . hokum though it may be" (p. 95).

John Cawelti's approach is not as hagiographical. He deals largely with Fleming's social impact as a novelist. In his own words, Fleming's importance is in his "position in the history of the spy story as reincarnation of the heroic spy created by John Buchan and his contemporaries" (*The Spy Story,* p. 126). Nor is Cawelti so ready to accept Fleming's attitudes toward sex and country as uncritically as does Amis. Fleming is, in Cawelti's opinion, an anachronism in the tradition of the heroic spy story popularized by John Buchan and his contemporaries.

Fleming's secret service is still unwaveringly on the side of truth, justice, and the British way. In *From Russia, with Love* (p. 41), the head of the Communist secret service (General "G") says of the British security service:

Their agents are good. They pay them little money . . . but they serve with devotion. . . . Their social standing is not high, and their wives have to pass as the wives of secretaries. They are rarely awarded a decoration until they retire. And yet the men and women continue to do this dangerous work. It is perhaps the Public School and University tradition. The love of adventure. But still it is odd that they play this game so well, for they are not natural conspirators.

Our own interpretation takes as one of its basic premises the conviction that—despite the assertions of some of his wartime colleagues that Fleming had a vivid imagination—his fiction-writing was not remarkably innovative or creative. He did not slavishly take characters and episodes unaltered from his life experience, but nearly all of those he did take seem to have been only slightly modified. It is our belief that his novels are largely psychological projections of himself, and that their plots are expressive extensions of Fleming's relations during early childhood with his mother, his older brother, and his absent father.

Ideally, we would want to know more about his mother, Evelyn

Rose, particularly how she was raised by her mother, how these two women related to each other. The Fleming family had an intergenerational lack of warmth; understanding Ian's mother's relationship with her own mother would clarify some areas. But it has not been possible to obtain that information, and so our analyses will be somewhat speculative. We cannot be certain of her relationship with her son, though about this there is some evidence, however anecdotal. Unknown factors include the manner of Ian's breastfeeding and toilet training, particularly the generosity or harshness with which both were carried out. Our guess, based on observations of others of the mature Fleming, is that Evelyn was not a generous or nurturing mother. If she did breastfeed him, it was not sufficient to satisfy his emotional needs: she was not emotionally available to him. We do know, from a number of sources, that she favored Peter. He could do almost nothing wrong, while Ian in early years could do nothing right.

Women's breasts are always mentioned—and usually described—in the Bond novels. We know that they are "firm," or "hard," "beautiful," "fine," "splendid," "jutting" with pride. Fleming concentrates on women's breasts as on no other part of their body; breasts became for him the synecdochic symbol of the whole being. Such heavy attention suggests an unrequited need. A mother who might be conflicted about or ungenerous about breastfeeding would probably also be overly anxious about toilet training, fastidious and eager to train at an early age. Early and rigorous toilet training often accompanies early weaning. Both arouse in the infant a discomfort with sensuality. Babies who are breastfed and receive emotional satisfaction from the experience establish a pattern for their later years. For instance, in a man's relations with women a pattern of comfort and pleasure is established. Nothing in Fleming's biography indicates close or comfortable emotional relations with anyone—women or men. An isolated figure, he corresponded closely to Horney's description of the detached personality. The emphasis on women breasts, the frequent baths and showers (the author's and Bond's) point to an uncomfortable infancy.

Everything in the mother's behavior indicates a narcissistic and self-centered person. Her own family had been very concerned about the appearance of things in their lives—a characteristic of families with pretensions to social prominence but without great wealth. Never having quite enough money to be wealthy, they had to worry constantly about how things looked in order to maintain the appearance of social status. Having married well, Evelyn Fleming strove to maintain the status of the family through her sons' achievements, with a special focus on how things looked to the external world. This would help explain the fact that Fleming is primarily a novelist of surfaces, seldom getting into his characters' psyches. His approach reflected his mother's whole way of thinking—about society, her life, and all of their lives within English society.

We do not know, but we can guess, that even after Ian was born, his other brother Peter retained a favored position in his mother's esteem. Usually the new baby displaces the older sibling in its mother affections, and becomes at least the temporary focus of the mother's adoration. The situation among Ian, Peter, and their mother suggests that Ian may not have been deeply wanted.

Fleming does not seem at any time in his childhood to have been exposed to a parental figure who imparted much emotional depth. Because he lost his father early, Ian Fleming never enjoyed the benefit of his love and influence. Even before Valentine Fleming went to war, his social and political duties as M.P. from 1910 until 1917 kept him away from home. These duties began when Ian was only two; he went to war when Ian was six and died three years later. A child's ability to think realistically about the world develops around age seven; at that age the child is very open to role models (for instance, his first relatively profound thoughts about religion will occur at this time). At this crucial period of Ian's life, his father was at first frequently absent, and then dead. We have already mentioned the Adlerian view that the father tends to discourage the oldest child from receiving all of the family's affection. But there was no emotional buffer for the young Ian. Their mother's narcissistic orientation would inevitably become that of her sons as well.

Ian Fleming was left to struggle along as the black sheep who never quite fit in with his surroundings, in the role of the temperamental, "difficult" child—which he certainly was at Eton and Sandhurst, and then again at Tennerhof. If he was difficult from the beginning, he would have needed specific and correct emotional attention to help him develop. But in his early years, despite his manifestation of a number of aptitudes, he did not get this attention. He had almost no emotional allies during his early childhood. It was not until he was tutored by Forbes Dennis and Phyllis Bottome that he received any nurturing of his talents and capabilities. They seem to have been his first important emotional allies; before the Swiss experience, he was constantly being thrust into confrontational situations. He developed an oppositional stance, both toward his family of origin and his later "families" of acquired friends and acquaintances. A friend of the prewar years, Gerald Coke, wrote to John Pearson that though Fleming seemed to have everything he could possibly have wanted—looks, brains, money, social position—"he was never satisfied. He always behaved as if he were permanently deprived" (Pearson, p. 73).

Eton's influence was an extension of his mother's will. Ian was there because of her, and he was there to achieve for her. In the event, his outstanding achievements were in athletics—his brother Peter had already taken the prizes in the academic and intellectual "fields." Peter's success in writing at an early age prevented Ian from competing with him as a writer until he was more than forty years old. In nearly all families, each member assumes a well-defined role. Peter was the intellectual; Ian became the athlete. The field of intellectual accomplishment was ceded to Peter before a "contest" could take place. Ian does not seem to have had much alternative to the role he did choose for himself.

He also wrapped himself in the mantle of the "bad boy" role—witness his difficulties at Eton and Sandhurst with automobiles and with women. Why would he take the "bad boy" role? It was better than no role at all, for such a role did give him something that he could do well, it did give him an identity, it did get him attention. A black sheep with panache, with style (played with some moderation, not radical enough to make the player irretrievably outcast) has a place within the family. Usually family members do not abandon the misfit because in some ways they can relate to him. Though a negative identity, it is nevertheless an acceptable substitute for no identity at all. Here was a well-established personality type that he could assume, an individuality that was easily available to him. The Byronic attitude— young Fleming's sulkiness, his fits of melancholy, his world-weariness—was a ready-made mask that suited his more encompassing role as black sheep. Peter was so wonderful, so stable; Ian, who from the first had trouble earning praise and empathy, was almost forced to choose another role.

Valentine Fleming was probably much idolized while he was still alive; we know that after his death he was memorialized as a hero. His virtues were almost certainly inflated. So, during the period when many sons first formulate role models for themselves based on what they perceive of their father's behavior, Ian had only written communications—letters and cards, not necessarily addressed to him. These, in his burgeoning imagination, would have served as the basis for adventures in his father's life at the Front, supplemented by what he heard about the war. In this way, without his mother's empathy, he could envision a heroic father engaging in valorous exploits and triumphs. A young boy could happily identify with this father, the father of his imagination.

Sending her son to Sandhurst seems typical of Mrs. Fleming's attitude toward her miscreant second son; it was about the worst place for Ian to be. The academy's strict discipline, had he stayed, would have been ruinous for him. And yet years later he often told friends that he had graduated and had actually received assignment to a regiment— the famed Black Watch. He would repeat that fantasy aspect of his life so often that it became indistinguishable from reality for him. An overwhelmingly strong need to see himself, and to be seen, as someone successful and strong, in the eyes of others as well as his own, led to this deception. He was not able to live with the person that he really was. That these deceptions of friends were carried on during Fleming's maturity suggests that he did not greatly value his writing achievements. Bond was, after all, just a "cardboard booby."

Thus we have our own variant interpretation of Pearson's and Storr's observations that Fleming's "collective villain-figure" bases his power on sources of adult superiority: extreme wealth, a source of power and a license for the practice of undiluted evil, and unbridled sexual appetites (Pearson, p. 197). As Pearson admits, this is more true of Le Chiffre than of any of the later villains. He "spoke like a father" to Bond several times; after him no one else ever did. And we believe that Fleming could have conceived of wealth as a source of evil from other origins; his own fear of poverty, for instance, owing to his being a second son. Or the Bible, where he might have learned that the love of money is the root of all evil.

Working as personal assistant to the director of Naval Intelligence was an ideal job for Ian. He could exploit and gain status through his gifts as a talented administrator, as his father was, and do many of the same things well (both the father's responsibilities as M.P. and his as assistant came at similar ages in their lives). Since his father's wartime heroics were for Ian largely imaginary, he could freely imagine a heroic role for himself: his exploits in invaded France, his direction of 30 Assault Unit, his suggestion that antiaircraft guns be mounted in frozen clouds. We recall that as a stockbroker—not an occupation that would give scope to heroism, imagined or real—he was a dismal failure.

It has long been acknowledged that there is a lot of schoolboy adventures in the Fleming novels. Ian was just entering puberty when his father left for the war. There is a frozen quality to the whole James Bond character: elements of the schoolboy; grandiose aspects that are semimagical; solutions based on power and clever intrigue. This reflects a preadult understanding of the way the world works and thus how one succeeds in it. One of the first of Fleming's controversial literary scenes occurs in *Casino Royale*; Le Chiffre, having captured Bond, ties him, naked, to a chair whose wicker seat has been cut out. And in order to get information from him, he strikes Bond with a carpetbeater on the hero's testicles. The scene is much like a prefect's room in a boy's school. It is also psychodrama. Bond's most private and most vulnerable bodily parts are exposed to the sadism of a powerful person, here in the position of adult to the schoolboy victim. The scene is a powerful expression of vulnerability to pain directly inflicted by a sadistic older person. Scenes of torture occur elsewhere in the Bond novels (*Doctor No*, for instance, and he endures great physical pain in *Moonraker*); in these scenes, and several others, Bond prevails not through any intelligence or cleverness or scheming of his, but because he endures this pain.

These scenes, it seems to us, recall Fleming's life with his mother, and probably also his early schooling when his sensibilities were ignored, not nurtured. Revealed most clearly in *Casino Royale,* this sense that life consists of torture at the hands of powerful people is a main theme in all the Bond books. For Fleming they inflicted emotional torture, constant assaults that he had to endure. Like Bond, who survived physical torture because he endured, Fleming would survive (in order to grow up) because he could endure constant emotional assaults. If one can get through a horrible childhood—symbolized by horrible physical tortures—one wins. One grows up. Growing up is the ultimate revenge on the parent figure.

In *Live and Let Die,* Bond and Solitaire are captured by Mr. Big and tied by a long rope to the stern of a fast boat. Mr. Big's plan is to drag the pair at speed over a coral reef, bloodying them so that sharks and barracuda in the area will be drawn to them and attack with their murderous fury. Bond, meanwhile, has been able to attach a limpet mine to the bottom of Mr. Big's boat, and before he can carry out his sadistic intentions, the mine explodes and his yacht sinks quickly to the bottom of the Caribbean. Some torture occurs before the boat explodes; Bond and Solitaire do not escape entirely unscathed, but they are able to cheat the sharks by swimming back to the safe side of the reef. The senselessness of the torture to which Bond and the woman are to be put is a prominent feature here. Once again the hero is able to endure, and to overcome an "older" figure, one who has him in his power. The scene suggests a painful childhood that held no possibility of rectifying the ongoing injustice—only survival, or outwitting the cause of the pain.

Equally significant is the use of ropes to secure Bond and Solitaire. Some infants are actually bound, others are physically confined in other ways; both are symbolized as rope binding. While Bond is making his way through Dr. No's tubular torture chamber, Honeychile Rider has been securely spreadeagled (with ropes!) on a mound in the known path of crabs who are to make their way to the top, devouring her on their way, the good doctor hopes. But on this occasion the crabs pass her by, possibly intent on more (or less?) appetizing fare. Bond later rescues her unharmed. Again, recollections of the infancy of the author seems to be evoked here. How the baby is handled in infancy can have long-lasting effects. The scene suggests (among several things) the diapering of a baby; and we recall that Honey is wearing a diaperlike garment around her loins (she is naked above the waist) when Bond first sees her. Primitive images of constricting devices—like the ropes in a number of the Bond novels—but also narrow tubes (in *Doctor No* and the missile silo in *Moonraker*) make us wish for more detailed knowledge of Fleming's early childhood. Would it explain his preoccupation with confinement, ropes, and narrow cylinders?

Readers of the Bond novels are struck by the hero's personal hygiene. He is continually bathing, washing, showering. In *Doctor No* he takes at least five baths and showers, including one shortly after he has been bruised and wounded by the torture tube he has just endured—and escaped from. No matter how tenderly Honeychile handles him, a shower at such a moment seems needlessly painful—unless the author has an obsession about washing. And we do remember Fleming's comments about the dirtiness of women, even American women: they could all use a good scrubbing. Storr cites a story (p. 19) in which Fleming "disowns" a girl to whom he was attracted because, while at the beach with him, she went behind a rock to urinate. Here again, analysts have found that excessive concern with cleanliness has its roots in toilet training. The child may have been made excessively aware of the risk of soiling. Feeling soiled involves a sense of being contami-

nated, perhaps by something obscene; such people are constantly washing their hands (or themselves) in order to be rid of the (symbolic)
disease or filth that has to be avoided or gotten rid of. This would
include certain feelings, especially guilt. Fleming's "extreme distaste"
for anything to do with excrement indicates that he was emotionally
arrested at Freud's anal-sadistic stage of development.

If Fleming's mother had responded to his soiling with expressions
of disgust, the frequent washing/showering is a way of warding off
guilt feelings all of his life—feelings of vulnerability, feelings of desire
for contact. The washing away of Bond's blood, caused by Dr. No's
diabolic machine, is evidence of Bond's/Fleming's desire to be rid of
all the evidence of his injuries (symbolic of psychic injuries).

Doctor No ends when Bond, forcing his way into a crane that is
loading guano onto a dockside boat, buries the villain under tons of
guano. (The scene was objectionable enough that it was altered in the
movie.) The psychological implications are strong and clear. Now,
guano is usually white in color, and we are reminded of the children's
rhyme:

> Birdie, birdie in the sky
> Dropped a white wash in my eye
> I won't weep and I won't cry
> But I'm sure glad that cows don't fly

Guano, being white, is both excremental and nutritive: it is a valued
fertilizer. As a symbol, therefore, it is the perfect expresser of confusion
about excrement and about milk, a nutrient. The villain's name points
us toward this symbol. The age at which children first start saying
"no" is about fifteen months, just a few months short of the time when
they gain control over their excretory functions. At this time they are
still orally oriented because they are still being breastfed or drinking
from a bottle. It seems reasonable to say, therefore, that *Doctor No*
describes a phase in Fleming's life which we commonly name separa-
tion and individuation—and emergence from an oral to a more controlled mode of being. It marks the transition from dependence to
independence, a phase in which the individual gains power over some
portions of life. Guano is thus the perfect symbol for the confusion
over the disgust we may feel over bodily functions, and recognition of
its power. In Fleming's early life, excrement represented his mother's

disgust toward bodily functions, but also his closeness to her, a desire for love characterized by closeness and trust and cooperation.

White snow does not figure as obviously in Fleming's writing as does guano, but water images do. Blofeld's alpine sanitarium is engulfed in snow. When the snow is melted and becomes water it is symbolically significant. The Bond novels are full of water imagery: Mr. Big's boat and the Caribbean, Largo's yacht (in *Thunderball*) on the same sea, Dr. No's island, Blofeld's magical island in *You Only Live Twice*, the ocean setting of "Risico" and "The Hildebrand Rarity." Water is one of the most common maternal symbols known. And the use of this common uterine symbol, juxtaposed with danger as it usually is in Fleming, suggests again a hostile mother. And the fact that Fleming's mother ran the family from 1914 on (if not before) further reinforces an interpretation of Fleming's symbols as antagonistic to her, as revelatory of his painful early life with her. Whether he was at home or away at school, his mother always meddled in his life.

The vulnerable, imperiled, apparently helpless, and attractive woman is a staple of Fleming's writing. Such women are almost the antithesis of his mother—who was not helpless, not vulnerable, not soft—and so would appear to be an example of wish fulfillment. Such a woman—Vesper Lynd, Solitaire, Jill Masterson, Honeychile Rider, Kissy Suzuki, etc.—is an image of the women Fleming would want to meet—and often enough did—and master. Fleming did not have a sister, and so he did not grow up with a female role model other than his mother. The females of the Bond fiction embody aspects of womanhood that he did not find in his mother; they represent split-off aspects of the ideal mother (the good aspects, rather than the bad). Always beautiful, young, responsive to him, Fleming's heroines inevitably have "fine" breasts. They are not only sexual fantasies but also fantasies of the ideal mother. Bond marries only one woman in all of the novels—Tracy Vicenzo—and she is killed off almost immediately. Thus Fleming saves his hero from marrying a mother-figure, and saves his fictionalized projection from hated entanglements. Since Fleming's women represented the good mother, Bond could never be permitted to marry one of them. Little boys can possess their mothers, but they cannot live in wedlock with them.

The most obvious symbol of Fleming's conflict over his own sexuality is James Bond's fascination with guns. A key scene occurs in *Doctor*

No. Bond's commander, "M," calls him into his office to brief him on a new mission, but also to order a change of armament for him. James is to turn in his .25 Baretta that has served him faithfully for fifteen years. It has never jammed or misfired and, Bond points out, it has never missed its target. But Major Boothroyd, the special armorer for the Secret Service pronounces the Baretta a "ladies' gun." Bond is more than slightly discomfited; his eyes show irritation. But it is no use; "M" had decided. Asked by "M" what he recommends, Boothroyd pedantically replies, "Of all of them, I'd choose the Walther PPK 7.65 mm. It only came fourth after the Japanese M-14, the Russian Tokarev and the Sauer M-38. But I like its light trigger pull and the extension spur of the magazine gives a grip that should suit 007. It's a real stopping gun."

When "M" asks about "something bigger," Boothroyd immediately says "there's only one gun for that, sir . . . Smith and Wesson Centennial Airweight. Revolver. .38 calibre. Hammerless, so it won't catch in clothing. . . ." "M" makes a perfunctory pass at sympathy to Bond: "I know how you like that bit of iron. But I'm afraid it's got to go." This exchange of guns is clearly a traumatic experience for Bond: ". . . he had the ties [to the gun] and M was going to cut them" (1958, pp. 18–21).

Beyond the obvious equation of the gun with the penis lies a psychic matter: Fleming's projection of his infant fantasies. Bond is ordered to put aside his "ladies'" gun for one that is more powerful. The Baretta is small, the Smith and Wesson (and the Walther) is bigger, more potent. Bond is, at this moment, being thrust into a more mature stage of manhood; he is being ordered to put by his childhood self and to move on to a more adult phase of life. Reluctantly, he discards his sense of himself as a boy and adopts the power of a man.

Much of Fleming's early life predicts an insecure, limited, exploitative, even despicable adult. He exploited women cold-heartedly, was often superficial in his relationships with both men and women, and endlessly pursued his own gratification. But that is not the whole impression we wish to leave. We also see him as a man who, considering his emotionally deprived childhood, the fact that he got little emotional nourishment before he was tutored by Forbes Dennis and Phyllis Bottome (at age nineteen), managed a great deal with the psychic resources that fell to him.

Fleming was able, from the Swiss experience on, to fashion a creative life out of very meager beginnings. He sublimated unfulfilled yearnings in fiction that entertained millions of others. Out of a lifelong feeling that he was probably a failure (apart from his early wartime experience), Fleming created a character of international renown. From worse than nothing, he became productive. Out of his most deeply felt conflicts, he wrote books that made millions of readers empathize with those struggles and see in them something of their own lives,

It is easy to moralize about Fleming's adult life, easy to be critical or judgmental; we want to understand the adult Fleming, to see his actions as perhaps the only possible ones given his childhood and youth. That he was unable to create characters with an inner life of their own reflects his own childhood, when he was misunderstood and emotionally undernourished. Lack of empathy for the characters in his novels is the result of a childhood in which no empathy was directed toward him.

Fleming was able to develop his innate gifts—personal charm, the ability to make friends easily, the ability to write rapidly and clearly. Within the British societal structure of his lifetime, he advanced his career, his social standing, and the sales of his book (though by methods that would not seem quite sporting to egalitarian Americans). Erick Erickson sees the last developmental stage of adult life as a choice between integrity and despair. In the last few years of his life, when the Bond books and the movies had become a "phenomenon," he defended his writing against his critics. This was a healthy sign, much more positive than his self-deprecatory "cardboard booby" remarks. We see Fleming in his last years coming to terms with himself, accepting his life as the only possible course that he could have taken. Out of an enormous pain, he produced more than a dozen books that have brought pleasure to millions of readers.

Works Cited

PRIMARY WORKS

Fleming, Ian. *Casino Royale.* 1953; New York: Berkley, 1983.
———. *Doctor No.* 1958; New York: Berkley, 1985.
———. *Diamonds Are Forever.* 1956; New York: Berkley, 1983.
———. *For Your Eyes Only.* 1959; New York: Berkley, 1985.
———. *From Russia, with Love.* 1957; New York: Berkley, 1983.
———. *Goldfinger.* 1959; New York: Berkley, 1983.
———. *Live and Let Die.* 1954; New York: Berkley, 1984.
———. *The Man with the Golden Gun.* 1965; New York: New American Library, 1966.
———. *Moonraker.* 1955; New York: Berkley, 1984.
———. *On Her Majesty's Secret Service.* 1963; New York: New American Library, n.d.
———. *The Spy Who Loved Me.* 1962; New York: Berkley, 1983.
———. *Thunderball.* 1961; New York: Berkley, 1984.
———. *You Only Live Twice.* 1964; New York: New American Library, n.d.

SECONDARY WORKS

Amis, Kingsley. *The James Bond Dossier.* New York: New American Library, 1965. Intelligent, witty, controversial defense of Fleming's work. Full of details and analyses.
Anon. "Bond's Creator." *New Yorker,* 21 April 1962, 32–34. Revealing personal insights.
Anon. "The Bond Phenomenon." *Newsweek,* 19 April 1965, 95–96. Useful for understanding contemporary reaction.
Antonini, Fausto. "The Psychoanalysis of 007." In del Buono and Eco, 103–21. Intelligent and insightful, anticipates nearly all such subsequent criticism.
Barbato, Andrea. "The Credible and the Incredible in the Films of 007." In del Buono and Eco, 133–45. Interesting criticism, but of the films, none of which were written by Fleming.

Benson, Raymond. *The James Bond Bedside Companion*. New York: Dodd, Mead & Co, 1984. Superficial, adoring, but entertaining.

Boyd, Ann S. *The Devil With James Bond!* Richmond: John Knox Press, 1967. Intelligent though debatable evaluation of the Bond novels from an ecclesiastical perspective, concerned almost exclusively with the philosophical aspects of ennui.

Bryce, Ivar. *You Only Live Twice*. Frederick, Md.: University Publications of America, 1982. Interesting insights into Fleming's life recalled by a friend.

del Buono, Oreste and Umberto Eco. *The Bond Affair*. Translated by R. A. Downie. London: MacDonald, 1966. Collection of essays, many good, including the first mature considerations of the Bond novels.

Calisi, Romano. "Myths and History in the Epic of James Bond." In del Buono and Eco, 76–85. Intelligent discussion of the subject mentioned in its title.

Cawelti, John and Bruce Rosenberg. *The Spy Story*. Chicago: University of Chicago Press, 1987. Insightful, dispassionate analysis of the important Bond novels by a leading critic.

Colombo, Furio. "Bond's Women." In del Buono and Eco, 86–102. Anticipates nearly all subsequent criticism of this important subject.

Connolly, Cyril. *Previous Convictions*. London: Hamish Hamilton, 1963. The generous criticism of a friend.

Deighton, Len. *Yesterday's Spy*. New York: Warner Books, 1975.

Delmer, Sefton. *Black Boomerang*. 2 vols. London: Secher and Warburg, 1962. Remembrance of World War II days.

Daly, Michael. "I Spy." *New York*, 6 April 1987, 34–47. Useful for contemporary appraisals of the Bond phenomenon.

Eco, Umberto. "The Narrative Structure in Bond." In del Buono and Eco, 35–75. One of the most stimulating appraisals of the Bond novels by a major critic.

Fleming, Ann. *The Letters of Ann Fleming*. Edited by Mark Amory. London: Collins Harville, 1985. An invaluable resource for any understanding of Fleming's personal life, as well as a perceptive look into Ann.

Gant, Richard. *Ian Fleming: The Man With the Golden Pen*. London: Mayflower-Dell, 1966. Slight, superficial, heavily reliant on Pearson's biography.

Gardner, John. *The Dancing Dodo*. New York: Bantam, 1985.

Greene, Graham, *The Human Factor*. New York: Simon and Schuster, 1978.

———. *Ways of Escape*. New York: Penguin Books, 1981.

Harling, Robert. "The Ian Flemings." *Vogue*, 1 September 1965, 222. Interesting personal glimpses by an old friend.

Holbrook, David. *The Masks of Hate*. Oxford: Pergamon Press, 1972. A hostile view of what the author sees as Fleming's antisocial aspects.

Horney, Karen. *Our Inner Conflicts.* New York: W. W. Norton, 1945.

Johnson, Paul. "Sex, Snobbery and Sadism." *New Statesman,* 5 April 1958, 430. This severely critical article has become famous, only in part because it wounded the Flemings personally.

Kettle, Michael. *Sidney Reilly.* New York: St. Martins, 1983. One of the few scholarly biographies of the famous spy, necessarily disappointing because so little about him can be firmly established.

Le Carré, John. *Call for the Dead.* New York: Popular Library, 1961.

Lilli, Laura. "James Bond and Criticism." In del Buono and Eco, 146–71. An early and now out-of-date compendium.

Lockhart, Robin Bruce. *Reilly: Ace of Spies.* New York: Penguin Books, 1984. A popular, often conjectural biography of the famous spy by the son of one of Reilly's collaborators.

McCormick, Donald. Personal correspondence with the authors. November 1987.

McLachlan, Donald. *Room 39: A Study in Naval Intelligence.* New York: Atheneum, 1968. A reminiscence of World War II days by a former Intelligence agent.

Panek, LeRoy L. *The Special Branch: The British Spy Novel, 1890–1980.* Bowling Green: BGU Popular Press, 1981. An interesting critical book with much valuable information, often conjectural—and often wrong.

Pearson, John. *The Life of Ian Fleming.* London: Jonathan Cape, 1966. The standard work on Fleming's life, written by a former colleague, to which all subsequent studies respectfully and correctly refer.

Philby, Kim. *My Silent War.* New York: Ballantine Books, 1983. A self-defense of his life by the former officer of SIS and KGB agent.

Pincher, Chapman. *Too Silent Too Long.* New York: St. Martins, 1984.

Rubin, Steven Jay. *The James Bond Films.* New York: Arlington House, 1981. An adoring glance at the films and their makers.

"Sapper." *Bull-Dog Drummond. His Four Rounds With Carl Peterson.* London: Hodder and Stoughton, 1929. A likely Fleming source.

Sauder, Ron. "The Clandestine Muse." *Johns Hopkins Magazine* August 1986, 11–16. An interview with John Le Carré.

Sauerberg, Lars Ole. *Secret Agents in Fiction.* New York: St. Martins, 1984. A look at the major spy writers by an intelligent and knowledgeable critic.

Snelling, O. F. *Double 0 Seven James Bond: A Report.* London: Neville Spearman, Holland Press, 1964. A slight study of the character and affectations of James Bond.

Stevenson, William. *A Man Called Intrepid.* New York: Ballantine, 1976. A largely fictionalized account of the wartime adventures of Sir William Stephenson, who knew Fleming.

Storr, Anthony. *The Dynamics of Culture.* New York: Atheneum, 1985. A psychological discussion of the creative process.

Tanner, William. *The Book of Bond*. New York: Viking, 1965. Slight, out-of-date discussion of Fleming's hero.

Tornabouni, Lietta. "A Popular Phenomenon." In del Buono and Eco, 13–34. An early European appraisal of Bond's popularity on the Continent.

Usborne, Richard. *Clubland Heroes*. London: Constable, 1953. Invaluable, intelligent, witty discussion of the popular books of Buchan, "Sapper," and Yates. Usually cited by every writer on this interesting subject.

Van Dover, J. Kenneth. *Murder in the Millions*. New York: Frederick Unger, 1984. A harsh discussion (and condemnation) of the pernicious aspects of the works of Fleming and others.

West, Nigel. Personal correspondence with the authors. Fall 1987.

Zorzoli, G. B. "Technology in the World of James Bond." In del Buono and Eco, 122–32. Useful but now dated study of Bond as a modern, technological man.

Index

Adler, Alfred, 11, 13
Adventures of Sidney Reilly, The, 61
Ambler, Eric, 71, 77, 79, 82
Amis, Kingsley, 38, 49, 50, 67, 78, 88, 90, 94, 106, 123–25
Amory, Mark, xii, 4, 12, 20, 122
Antonini, Fausto, 62
Arbuthnot, Sandy, 42, 119
Avon, Clarissa, 6

Barthes, Roland, 85
Berlin Game/Mexico Set/London Match, 72, 79
Birch, Harvey, 76
Birds of the West Indies, 5
Black Shrike, The, 67
Blofeld, Ernst Stavros, 39, 46, 54, 77, 80, 81, 87, 95, 99, 102, 116–17, 118, 121, 123, 133
Bond, James (ornithologist), 5, 21
Bond, James, 5, 7, 8, 12, 17, 22, 30, 34, 36, 37, 40, 41–47, 50–52, 54, 55, 59, 61–66, 68–71, 77–84, 91, 93, 94, 100, 102, 103–5, 106, 112, 116, 118–21, 123, 130–33
Booth, Wayne, 51–52
Boothroyd, Maj., 134
Bottome, Phyllis, 1, 13, 14, 127, 134
Broccoli, Albert, 7–9, 21, 51, 68, 86
Brownrigg, Philip, 6
Bryce, Ivar, 15, 16
Buchan, John, 41–44, 51, 54, 71, 74–77, 80, 104, 119, 120, 125
Bunt, Irma, 95, 101, 118
Byronic stance (posture, image), 1, 14, 16

Call For the Dead, 64
Camp "X" (at Oshawa, Canada), x, 36
Case, Tiffany, 95, 97, 102, 112
Casino Royale, 7, 12, 21, 34, 35, 38–41, 44, 50, 52, 55, 59, 78, 88, 96, 99, 101, 106, 117, 130
Cawelti, John, xii, 46, 51, 52, 119, 121, 125
Chandler, Raymond, 22–23, 119
CHEKA, 58
Childers, Erskine, 73, 75, 76, 78
Churchill, Sir Winston, 11, 27, 29, 37, 73
Colonel Sun, 67
Confidential Agent, The, 71–72
Connery, Sean, ix, 9, 85, 86
Connolly, Cyril, 3
Conrad, Joseph, 74–76
Cooper, James Fenimore, 72–73, 75, 76
Coward, Noel, 18, 22, 46, 121
Cuneo, Ernest, 11, 12, 18, 23

Dahl, Roald, 8
Dalton, Timothy, ix, 68
Deighton, Len, 50, 54, 62, 69, 79, 81–83
Delmer, Sefton, 2–3, 29
Dennis, Forbes, 1, 13–15, 127, 134
Diamonds Are Forever, 6, 79, 89, 92, 102, 112
Doctor No, 7, 8, 19, 22, 36, 39, 50, 67, 78, 79, 89, 90, 100, 102, 114, 115, 123, 130–34
Doctor No (fictional character), 47, 54, 87, 95, 98, 114–16, 118, 131–33
Double O Seven James Bond: A Report, 124
Drax, Hugo, 31, 40, 44, 45, 48, 77, 80, 87, 92, 95, 97, 98, 108, 110, 111, 123
Drummond, Bulldog, 38, 41–44, 71, 78, 80, 81, 83, 87, 109, 123, 124

Eco, Umberto, 38, 40, 41, 45, 48, 49, 50, 87, 93, 94, 95, 113
Eton, 1, 5, 12, 13, 15, 21, 43, 46, 52, 64, 65, 120, 121, 127, 128

Fairy Tale (fictional structure), 95–96
Feldman, Charles, 7
Fleming, Ann (Charteris), xii, 4, 7, 9,
    17, 19, 20, 22, 104, 122
Fleming, Evelyn St. Croix Rose, 11, 14,
    15, 17, 125–27, 129, 133
Fleming, Peter, 1, 10–13, 56, 120,
    126–28
Fleming, Robert, 10, 11, 25
Fleming, Valentine, 11, 127, 128
For Your Eyes Only, 80
From Russia, With Love, 7–9, 45, 48,
    78, 79, 89, 98, 101, 102, 112, 117,
    118, 125

Galore, Pussy, 54, 95, 98, 122
Gardner, John, 63, 65, 66, 69, 81
Godfrey, Adm. John H., 24, 25, 28,
    30, 32, 34, 59
Goldeneye, 5, 18, 20, 21
Goldfinger, x, 7–9, 22, 36, 44–46, 48–
    49, 78–79, 83, 85, 88, 93, 96–98,
    100, 112, 114, 121, 122
Goldfinger (fictional character), 54, 77,
    80, 87, 90, 94–95, 100, 108, 112,
    113, 118, 123
Goldman, William, 83
Grant, "Red," 49, 98, 108, 112
Greene, Graham, x, 41, 65, 71, 77,
    80, 82, 83

Hall, Adam, 62, 67, 79
Hall, Sir Reginald "Blinker," 24, 25
Hamilton, Donald, 69
Hannay, Richard, 38, 42, 43, 71, 74–
    76, 78, 80, 81, 87
Hardy, Thomas, 14
Harling, Robert, 33
Hart, Al, 7
Harwood, Joanna, 8
"The Hildebrand Rarity," 133
Hiss, Alger, 8
Holbrook, David, 120–22
Honorable Schoolboy, The, 72
Hoover, J. Edgar, 37, 61
Horney, Karen, 16, 126
Human Factor, The, x, 83

"Imaginary War Novels", 72–73
Ipcress File, The, 54
Istanbul, 23, 30

James Bond Dossier, The, 123
James Bond Island, 85
John of Gaunt, 11
Johnson, Paul, 119

Kaplan, Dora, 57
Kemsley newspapers, 3
Kennedy, Pres. John F., 6, 7, 50, 58
Kennedy, Robert, 6
KGB, 58, 69
Kitzbuhel, 4, 13
Klady, Leonard, 28, 85
Klebb, Rosa, 47, 95, 101, 117, 118
Knightley, Philip, 26, 28, 33, 84

Leamas, Alec, ix, 54, 65, 69, 80
Le Carré, John (David Cornwell), 16,
    25, 38, 41, 50, 54, 62–66, 69, 71,
    72, 77, 79, 82, 84, 109
Le Chiffre, 34, 87, 95, 106–11, 129,
    130
Leiter, Felix, 34, 43, 46
Lenin, Vladimir Ilyich, 57
Life of Ian Fleming, The, xii
Littell, Robert, 50, 52, 62, 69
Live and Let Die, 6, 7, 22, 36, 45, 79,
    88, 92, 97, 101–2, 109, 119, 120,
    130
"Living Daylights, The," 28, 68
Lockhart, Robin Bruce, x, 55, 56, 58,
    59
Lynd, Vesper, 95, 97, 99, 101, 133

"M," 88, 109–11, 134
Maibaum, Richard, 8
Maclean, Alistair, 67–68
"Man From UNCLE, The," 68
Mankiewicz, Tom, 8
Man with the Golden Gun, The, 8, 85
Marlowe, Philip, 62
Mask of Hate, The, 120–21
Maugham, W. Somerset, 22, 55, 71,
    78, 121

McCormick, Donald (Richard Deacon),
   xii, 3, 55, 56, 59
McGoohan, Patrick, 68
McLachlan, Donald, 27–29
Merritt, Edward, 29, 31
Mr. Big, 39, 54, 80, 87, 95, 109–11,
   113, 130, 133
Moonraker, 6, 17, 19, 40, 43, 45, 88,
   89, 93, 96, 110–12, 130, 131
Moore, Roger, ix, 51
Moravia, Alberto, 50, 93, 95

Naval Intelligence, Office of (Director
   of), 21, 55–56, 60, 129
No. 30 Assault Unit, 31–33, 129

Oakes, Boysie, ix, 66
Oddjob, 68, 90, 113
On Her Majesty's Secret Service, 38–39,
   81, 98, 102, 109, 117–18

Palmer, Harry, ix, 69
Pan Book Oscar, 9
Panek, LeRoy, 5
Pearson, John, ix, xii, 3, 14, 30, 41,
   45, 52, 128–29
Personal Assistant to the DNI, 24, 30,
   33
Philby, Kim, x, 8, 25, 58, 82, 84
Plomer, William, 5
Popov, Dusko ("Tricycle"), 55, 59–62

Quain, Sir Richard, 11
Quarrel, 47, 119
Quiller, ix, 67, 80

Racism, 87–95
Ratoff, Gregory, 7
Reilly, Sidney, x, xi, 2, 55–59, 61–62
Reilly: Ace of Spies, x, 55
Reilly: The First Man, 58
Reuters, 2, 56
Riddle of the Sands, The, 73
Rider, Honeychile, 95, 98, 100, 103,
   115, 131, 133
"Risico," 133

Room 39, 29, 30
Rushbrooke, Cmdr. E.G.N., 28, 32

Saltzman, Harry, 7–9, 21, 51, 86
Samson, Bernie, 54, 69, 80
Sandhurst, 1, 13, 21, 121, 127–29
"Sapper" (H. C. McNeil), 41–44, 51,
   54, 71, 77–78, 80, 104, 120
Second Oldest Profession, The, 26
Secret Agent, The, 74
Serocold, Sir Claude, 25
Sexism, 95–105
Sisters, The, 52
Skorzeny, Otto, 31
SMERSH, 44, 79–80, 108–9, 112,
   114, 117, 122
Smiley, George, 54, 65–66, 69, 79–80,
   84, 109
Snelling, O. F., 124–25
Solitaire, 95, 102, 110, 130, 131, 133
Spade, Sam, 62
SPECTRE, 79, 80
Spillane, Mickey, 38–39
Spy, The, 72
Spy Counterspy, 61
Spy Story, 54
Spy Story, The, 46, 119, 125
Spy Who Came in from the Cold, The, 65
Spy Who Loved Me, The, 78–79, 86
Stephenson, Sir William, x, 30, 34–36,
   39, 84
Stevenson, William, 6
Storr, Anthony, 120–21, 123, 129, 131
Suzuki, Kissy, 95, 133

Tambach, 33
Tennerhof, 1, 14, 21
Thirty-Nine Steps, The, 43, 74, 76
Three Days of the Condor, 72
Thrilling Cities, 6
Thunderball, 8, 22, 48, 67, 81, 98,
   101, 109, 116–17, 133
Trevanian, 67
Trevor-Roper, Hugh, 26

Usborne, Richard, 42–43, 118

Van Dover, J. Kenneth, 119, 121
Vicenzo, Tracy, 98–99, 103, 133
Vitale, Domino, 48, 95, 98, 101

Waugh, Evelyn, 6, 9, 13, 17, 22
West, Nigel, xii, 34, 61, 87
Wright, Peter, 84

Yanos, Dr. Janet, xii
Yates, Dornford, 42, 44, 51, 54
Young, Terence, 93
You Only Live Twice, 39, 47, 91, 109,
    117, 121, 133

Zinoviev letter, 57